INTERIOR SPACE

INTERIOR SPACE

Design Concepts for Personal Needs

Stuart Miller
& Judith K. Schlitt

PRAEGER

Westport, Connecticut
London

Library of Congress Cataloging-in-Publication Data

Miller, Stuart, 1940–
  Interior space.

  Bibliography: p.
  Includes index.
  1. Interior decoration – Psychological
aspects.   I. Schlitt, Judith K.   II. Title.
NK2113.M5   1985   728'.01'9   85-6337
ISBN 0-275-92824-1 (alk. paper)

Library of Congress Catalog Card Number: 85-6337
ISBN: 0-275-92824-1

First published in 1985

Praeger Publishers, One Madison Avenue, New York, NY 10010
A division of Greenwood Press, Inc.

Printed in the United States of America

The paper used in this book complies with the Permanent
Paper Standard issued by the National Information Standards
Organization (Z39.48-1984).

P

*This book is dedicated to
my parents Charles and Ida Miller,
my wife Carol, and my daughter Meredith
S.M.
and to Robert, Melinda, and a few special friends
whose encouragement has sustained me
J.K.S.*

ACKNOWLEDGMENTS

This book could not have been written without the help of others. We wish to express our appreciation to our editor George P. Zimmar, who recognized the value of our approach, encouraged us to present it to the professional design community, and supported us throughout our work. We wish to thank the many people whose residential interviews helped us explain the design concepts used in the book. The contributions of the following individuals, who assisted in the collection of data in various ways, are specifically recognized: Gail Kruggel, Cynthia Lindsay, Ann I. Santangelo, and Lori Miner. We are also grateful to Helene Shiffman for her patient typing and retyping of the manuscript. A special word of thanks is given to administrators and colleagues at Towson State University who supplied us with the time, the facilities, and the support needed to complete this project.

CONTENTS

INTRODUCTION

— 1 —

This book represents an attempt to apply research and theory from the field of environmental psychology to the design of private residential interiors. We hope that, through our efforts, homes will be designed to fit the individual psychological needs of residents. But before we discuss the specifics of our psychological need-satisfaction approach to design, we would like to talk about some of the defining characteristics of environmental psychology.

We define environmental psychology as the study of the interaction between people (their behavior and experience) and environments (built and natural). The environment affects us: it affects what we think, feel, and do. But, at the same time, we actively influence the environment in the process of using it to satisfy our needs.

It would appear from this definition that environmental psychology is potentially useful to environmental design practitioners in helping them to understand the behavioral and experiential implications of their design activities and modify their behavior accordingly. And, in fact, environmental psychological principles have been successfully applied to the design of large-scale public/semi-public places such as institutional settings (for example, hospitals and schools), work settings, recreational environments (for example, hiking trails and children's playgrounds), and cities themselves.

On the other hand, applications in the private interior residential sector have lagged behind these areas. The excellent research on housing has been applied typically to the design of public housing projects and university residence environments, settings in which residents are unknown to designers and turnover is often rapid. Consequently, practitioners have usually relied upon general principles and have designed for the "average" person. Our approach, however, is an individualized one, concerned with the creation of interiors that fit the specific needs of a small number of known residents in a most significant environment—the private home.

In fact, we feel very strongly that the home is the logical place for the enlightened intervention of interior designers because of the importance of this environment to the individual. But why is the home so important to people? According to Stokols (1976), the home is an example of a primary environment—a place in which we engage "in a wide range of personally-important activities" (p. 73). All of the basic human needs are satisfied there, including individual ones (for example, self-esteem and autonomy) and social ones (for example, love and affection). Although we are likely to have more control over events in the home environment than in secondary settings (for example, transportation and recreation), the failure to exercise control in the home threatens our emotional well-being as a number of personally important needs go unsatisfied.

Consequently, we decided to concentrate our efforts, as an interior designer/psychologist team, upon the home environment. As a first step, we thought that it was important to get a better understanding of the variety of needs that are satisfied there. We attempted to accomplish this goal by interviewing over a hundred people concerning their perceptions and recollections of significant home interior environments from the past, present, and future. We asked them a number of questions including the following:

> Describe, and give the location of, your important activities within the home. What significant experiences do you remember having there? Describe the feelings you have in each room. If this room could talk, what would it say to you, and how would it describe itself? What would your ideal home look like?

The analysis of the interview data proved to be quite fascinating and enlightening. When people talked about their experiences in the home, nine common themes were expressed. These themes corresponded closely to the psychological/social needs that have been studied by environmental psychologists. It was also clear that the satisfaction of these needs depended upon the nature and the quality of home interior design.

In order to provide you with a preliminary understanding of these needs, we will verbalize the thoughts and feelings of a hypothetical person talking about an ideal home environment. Each need is indicated in parentheses after its brief description in this fictitious narrative.

Because it is my home, I should have the ability to make changes in it when appropriate so that I can feel like an effective human being (control). I would prefer not to be disturbed, seen, or heard when I'm doing something in private (privacy). I would like to feel free to express my uniqueness as a person (identity). Certainly, I want to have a feeling of being safe and protected there (security). Things should be arranged in an orderly and organized fashion (order). My home should be interesting and stimulating; but, at the same time, it should also help me to relax (variety). I want my home to express my own definition of what is beautiful (aesthetics). When I'm there, I also want to experience a feeling of freedom of choice (choice). I would like my home to be a place where I can have satisfying relationships with guests, friends, and family members (sociability).

Thus, need-assessment is the first stage of our approach to the design of residential interiors. We conduct residential interviews, supplementing the questions we described previously with additional probes, in order to identify the dominant needs of the client(s). Although each of the nine needs has some degree of importance for all of us, interviews typically emphasize a small number of themes. Therefore, we have found it useful in simplifying the design process to concentrate on these dominant need-themes rather than to design for all of the needs at once.

Although proper interpretation of the data requires some knowledge of concepts in the field of environmental psychology, we think that designers who read this book can acquire some of the skills necessary to incorporate a need-assessment interview into their design practice. Toward that end, the nine environmentally related psychological needs are dimensionalized (that is, broken down into alternate forms, varieties, or components) in the next nine chapters. Available research is discussed. Interview examples and personal accounts are interpreted. Generally speaking, data, theory, hypothesis, personal observation, and personal experience are all combined to help the reader understand and interpret what people say about their home-environment experiences.

Once dominant needs are identified, they function as design goals for the designer and client. In other words, designers should make recommendations for the modification of the interior environment that help the client satisfy important needs. In this way, a person-environment fit is created; the environment is adjusted through design so that it is consonant with the needs of the client.

Of course, this task is not an easy one. In order to accomplish it, we must know what particular design elements, features, arrangements, compositions, etc. are relevant to the satisfaction of each need. Perhaps the major contribution of this book is to point out these potential links between need and design. Thus, we have developed a series of design concepts for each form of the nine psychological needs. Each concept synthesizes a number of different design features and represents an alternative way of satisfying a particular need-form through design. The conceptual nature of the design solutions presented in this book must be emphasized. In other words, our goal is to illustrate the process through which designs can be derived on the basis of environmental design research. Although we do present partial lists of specific design elements, they are not meant to be exhaustive. These lists are used as examples for concept definition and as stimuli for the designer's imagination.

It must also be emphasized that, in many cases, these design concepts are based upon untested applications of theories, personal hypotheses, and generalizations of data (sometimes from research on exterior environments). Our ideas need empirical verification, and we hope that psychologists who read this book will be stimulated to conduct such badly needed interior design research. However, we also think that although there is not yet an organized body of knowledge relating psychology to interior design, our attempt to provide a unifying framework rests on firm enough ground to begin some preliminary applications.

Although we expect this book will appeal to social scientists and students who are interested in applications of psychological concepts to interior design, our primary audience is the interior design practitioner. As such we would like to present some general guidelines concerning the use of this book in the practice of residential interior design.

1. Conducting the interview: Earlier we listed some suggested interview questions. However, we have found that the specific content of the items is not so important. People are extremely willing to discuss the satisfying and dissatisfying experiences they have had, are having, or would like to have in their homes. They are, in fact, pleased that we are so interested in them and fascinated by the process of creating designs that are based upon their unique experiences, feelings, and thoughts. These reactions are extremely helpful in establishing rapport with the client. There is one specific suggestion we have concerning interview content: We have found that it is better to focus upon the person (for example, feelings and attitudes) rather than upon the environment. We have learned much more about our clients by asking them to describe their experiences in the home

rather than to discuss what they like or dislike about the home itself. When people talk about themselves, the environmental context is naturally included; but when people discuss specific environmental preferences, underlying needs are not as clearly revealed.

2. Assessing needs: Before residential interviews are conducted, it would be worthwhile to become familiar with the nine psychological needs by thoroughly reading the appropriate sections of each of the following chapters. Later, interview responses can be compared with the definitions and examples contained in this book in order to increase the probability of proper need-interpretation. Again, we wish to emphasize this potentially complex process should be simplified as much as possible—at least initially. Concentrate on designing for a small number of dominant needs whose presence is made clear by the interview. However, there is also a danger of oversimplification. Try to avoid relying too much on labels for people (for example, this is a private person or this person needs relaxation) because needs vary from time to time for every person. Sometimes we want to be away from people; sometimes we want to be with them. Sometimes we like to relax; sometimes we like to be stimulated. Therefore, we have to be prepared to design for intra-person differences as well as inter-person differences. It is helpful to think of a need (for example, variety) as a continuum. Most of the time a person may prefer to remain in one part of that continuum (for example, the low end) and experience a restful and relaxing state. But occasionally this same person may wish to have the opposite experience (for example, excitement and stimulation). Our designs should be responsive to what is most characteristic of the person but should be flexible enough to take into account these need-shifts.

3. Dealing with families: Under ideal conditions, all household members should be involved in the interview/design process if they so choose. However, the collection of multiple interviews can increase the complexity of the interpretive problem. Again we have some advice to simplify this situation. We can always rely upon the universality of needs, as each of us would like to have control over the environment, have a positive self-identity, feel secure in our homes, etc. A better, but similar approach would be to look for specific areas of agreement among the interviews and use these common themes as the focus of our designs. For example, the following interview responses of one family that we worked with revealed a heavy emphasis upon order:

> *My ideal future home would be . . . easy to take care of. . . . Lots of hidden storage space, like little cubbyholes behind louvered*

doors, would be nice for keeping a cleared away look.

I don't like clutter. . . . I would like . . . things to go together well.

Plusses that I would like to attribute to our present home but can't are . . . organization, efficiency, and lack of clutter.

Things I dislike in my home are the clutter and unorganized sense of things. . . . It bothers me that . . . nothing's in order.

Therefore, our recommendations for a multi-purpose area designed for this family included the following: maintenance-free fabrics and surfaces, an existing closet with sliding doors utilized as concealed storage space, separate zones defined by clear boundaries, color coding, and various techniques (for example, lighting, color, and natural elements) to increase perceived spaciousness. Additionally, the differences between family members, which are often revealed in interviews, can be easily accommodated by either designing changeable environments that can be altered to suit the current user of the space or by creating separate, individualized spaces for each person. Generally speaking, we have found that the residential interview technique stimulates a healthy discussion among household members. As a result, an atmosphere of understanding and cooperation is established, the design process is simplified, and the success of the design intervention is enhanced.

4. Selecting design concepts: Once the design goals have been established (for instance, high-priority needs have been identified by the interview), appropriate chapters can be reviewed for relevant design concepts. We think that it is important to involve clients actively in the design-selection process and provide them with meaningful choices. Therefore, a large number of alternative solutions is presented for each variety of each need to fit variations in individual preferences and situational requirements. In some cases, the choice process can be simplified by looking for "creative solutions" that simultaneously satisfy several needs. Relevant examples are presented throughout this book (for example, bounded spaces that satisfy the need for control, security, and privacy). The adaptation of concepts to the specific living circumstances of the client is, of course, left up to the individual designer.

In conclusion, we have attempted to translate research and theory in environmental psychology into language that is understandable, and into a form that is usable, to those of us involved in the design of residential interiors. Our need-satisfaction approach represents a process to model so that our design behavior is directed, goal-oriented, responsive to client needs, and ultimately successful.

CONTROL

— 2 —

Psychologists have spoken of a basic motive to manipulate the environment in order to produce pleasant circumstances and avoid unpleasant ones. According to R.W. White (1959), satisfaction is derived from having an effect on the environment, changing it, and in general interacting with it successfully. We like to perceive ourselves as "Origins," people who produce effects and cause things to happen, rather than as "Pawns," people who are at the mercy of outside forces (deCharms, 1968). We call this motive the need for control.

We have chosen to discuss this need first because it is probably at the root of all other needs. In other words, if we lack control, it will be difficult to satisfy any of the other needs; but if we can bring the environment under our control, we can arrange things to serve our purposes. Unfortunately, in a complex urbanized society, we often encounter a variety of uncontrollable events—including traffic jams, lines, noise, pollution, bureaucracy, and crime—that threaten our sense of mastery over the environment. The home is the one place over which we do expect to have some control. However, even here the nature of the social environment and, most importantly for our purposes, the characteristics of the physical environment can interfere with our ability to control external events.

We hope that the concepts presented in this chapter will help designers avoid such an outcome in the homes they design. Then, people should be able to achieve control both behaviorally (that is, they can perform some response to modify the environment) and experientially (for instance, they will feel dominant, independent, important, and competent).

As you read through these design concepts keep one very important thing in mind: Client input at all stages of the design process is necessary for satisfying the need for control. This point is illustrated quite well by one of deCharms's (1968) experiments. In it, subjects preferred to design their own Tinker toy models rather than follow directions from the experimenter even though they thought the experimenter-directed model looked better.

Control of Space/Territoriality

We think that everyone in the household has the right to a place that is theirs—a personal territory. When people are in their own territory, they can stay there as long as they want, do whatever they want to do, design and arrange it any way they want, decide who shall have access to it, and direct the behavior of others. In short, having our own space gives us the opportunity to exert control over both the physical and the social environment, and experience a sense of mastery over our surroundings.

Many of our interviewees talked about the importance of territoriality, defined as the ownership, control, and occupation of space. So let's look very carefully at what they said about their home environments so that we may understand the various dimensions of this important concept and learn how to design the home accordingly.

[When I was young] I lived in a pink room. . . . I had fairly simple furnishings, posters on the wall, etc. . . . I did everything in my room except eat and bathe.

Analysis: As Edney (1976) points out, having no territory would quite literally mean that a person would be constantly milling around with no place to settle. This subject has a familiar, predictable, and comfortable territory to occupy.

I would like to have a lot of space so family members would have their own facilities. The master bedroom, bath, and study would be just for myself and my spouse. The children would have their own bathrooms. A spare bedroom and bath would be for guests.

Analysis: This subject would like to exercise territorial control over a variety of rooms, restrict access to these areas, and have separate spaces for other people.

When I was young my haven was my bedroom. Being upstairs, I had rule over four rooms. Sharing my territory is a fact of life now that my parents have moved to an old farmhouse. I'm definitely looking forward to having a bedroom that can be part sitting room, studio, and bed area.

Analysis: Notice how the need for control over space has developed over time. As a child, this subject was able to exert control over the upstairs of a two-story house. However, once the family moved to a different type of dwelling, the person was deprived of having a separate territory. Now a strong desire for territoriality in the future seems to be present.

In each of the preceding examples, people expressed a preference for having their own rooms; such an arrangement is desirable if there are enough rooms to go around. Parents should also be encouraged to recognize the often-ignored territorial rights of children; and that means not only giving children a room of their own, but also letting them do with it what they wish. (We'll have more to say about children's rooms later.)

However, many families live under conditions of spatial constraint; space must be shared. In fact, personal territories need not be completely separated from other areas of the house by walls, doors, etc. Instead, areas of personal control can be created by clearly defining their boundaries in other ways.

In order for a space to be perceived as a territory that belongs to someone, it must be easily differentiated from surrounding areas. One logical way to define space in this manner is to create clear, definite boundaries. Boundaries communicate to others—and to ourselves—where our place is, how big it is, where it begins, and where it ends.

Consider, for example, the following list of preferred places within the home mentioned by one of our subjects: an Oriental rug, a couch, a hot tub, a desk and chair surrounded by windows, a bed.

All of these places have one characteristic in common: They are all well bounded. They appealed to our subject because they are places in which he could experience a sense of personal control. He could engage in activities of his choosing with confidence within his bounded spaces. And he would be somewhat protected from the control of others because they would recognize that he is in a distinct, separate place even though they may still be able to see or hear him.

The following techniques, based on Zeisel's (1981) notion of barriers and fields, can be used to define territorial boundaries. Some of these mechanisms involve complete, or partial, physical separation, whereas others simply suggest the differentiation of space in a symbolic sense.

Enclosures

A number of choices are available for creating enclosures that people can enter to physically separate themselves from others within a shared space. Some environmental enclosures are manufactured. Alternatively, enclosed territories, with provisions for adequate ventilation, can be constructed (for example, a plywood cube or wooden frame with burlap, louvers, or translucent sliding panels for walls).

If the latter idea is adopted, it is desirable for clients to decide exactly what goes into the enclosure, a strategy that itself increases feelings of control. Some alternatives are as follows: a stereo, cassette player, radio or television set; an aquarium, a cage for a bird, a bed for a cat; a sun lamp; plants; a soft-textured floor of pillows, plush carpet, fur, or thin mattress. In any case, a personalized environment would be the goal.

This room-within-a-room not only provides its occupant with a strong, well-bounded territory, it also enables others to occupy the rest of the room comfortably without their sense of control being disturbed.

Finally, the enclosure concept can work quite well in combination with the bed. Beds can be enclosed with canopies and side draperies in the Tudor manner, or the sleeping area can be bounded by walls and entered through a sliding glass door.

Partitions

Panels, screens, counters, etc., which provide less physical separation than enclosures, can still be used effectively to define spatial zones. We have used this technique in a bedroom shared by two children. The room is divided into two distinct territories by a partition of cubes stacked in rows and anchored to each other by brackets. Smaller territories are provided underneath beds that are elevated off the floor. The boundaries of these spaces are controlled by other types of partitions (for example, draperies on tracks, which can be pulled ..cross the length of the bed, and shades, which can be lowered to cover the opening at the end of the bed). Furnishings, similar to the ones we devised, now exist as whole environments for children's bedrooms.

We have also used a natural partition of plants to define a territory within a multi-purpose room. In this case, seating was provided (a ceiling-suspended swing chair) inside a circular arrangement of plants in hanging baskets and small trees in tubs. Our client was then able to enjoy caring for her plants comfortably in her own bounded space within the larger area shared by the entire family. This space contributes to a feeling of control and can serve as a private sanctuary as well.

Objects

Things such as furniture, sculpture, and various structural elements influence the way people perceive space. For example, columns placed at the center of an otherwise open living space help us divide the area perceptually into two smaller, but related, zones.

In addition to acting as space dividers, stationary objects can also create a sense of place—a focal point of activity. For example, in our multi-purpose room, a work zone is defined by a desk, chair, and bookcase; and an entertainment area is created by the presence of a large piano. Additional examples of the use of objects to define territories are contained in later chapters as other needs are discussed: an indoor fountain to control acoustic privacy (Chapter 3) and heavy-looking furniture to produce a feeling of permanence (Chapter 5).

Shape

The shape of a room can be a perceptual cue for us to divide it into a series of smaller places rather than see it as a single space. The tendency to see corners as distinct places is illustrated by the following description of an ideal future home: "The area could be large at first impression; however, little oases or pockets of comfort would beckon around corners."

For this reason, the corners of a room provide excellent locations for individual territories. Our multi-purpose room, for example, contains a corner with a built-in bench; floor pillows would probably do just as well. Other configurations that perform the same function as corners are L-shapes, cloverleaves, and alcoves.

Elevation

Changes in floor levels and/or ceiling heights also serve as cues for territorial division. That's one reason why we chose bunk-style beds for the bedroom shared by two children. This decision was reinforced by one of the people we interviewed, who described how mattresses were used to elevate the bed. This strategy was employed in order to overcome feelings of crowding that could have resulted from sharing the bedroom with siblings.

We have also used platforms to define separate areas for eating, reading, and lounging in a basement designed for one of our clients. In the overhead dimension, the stairs provided a natural canopy, differentiating the phone area from the rest of the basement.

Light, Color, and Pattern

A variety of symbolic techniques can be used, in addition to elevation changes, to signal the ownership of space. Using a theatrical lighting model, areas can be selectively illuminated with task lights, spot lights on tracks, and dimming devices. Perimeter lighting can also be used to define the boundaries of a space (for example, a neon-tube border or a circle of ceiling or pendant lights).

Light and color can also be combined in different ways. For example, we defined individual territories with a tricolor neon-tube lighting system in a basement shared by three sisters. Each person chose a different color, which could be activated to signal possession of the occupied space. The colored-signal-light concept is developed further in Chapter 3 as a technique for regulating privacy.

Finally, areas can be color-coded or defined by distinctive patterns in area rugs, wallpaper, etc. In the children's bedroom that we described earlier, walls on either side of the cube barrier were done in different colors (for example, blue for one child and yellow for the other). The closet was also symbolically divided into two spaces by using each child's color. Similarly, the cube barrier itself consisted of both blue and yellow cubes, with the cubes of the child's color opening onto the child's side of the room for storage.

Control of the Ambient Environment

To get a better understanding of what kinds of things people would like to control in their homes, we asked a subset of our subjects to "design a room in which you have the ability to control different aspects of the environment."

The most striking thing about our data was that every one of our subjects wanted to control some aspect of the ambient environment. In other words, people seemed to be very concerned with controlling properties of the surrounding environment, such as temperature, air flow, sound, and light.

In considering ambient factors, we offer the following advice to designers: Don't limit your thinking to outcomes. Although it's important to create quality lighting, good acoustics, etc., you must also think of process—the process of control of the ambient environment. Clients should be supplied with a variety of controls—things to push and pull and turn and press and set. Manipulating these controls in order to produce desired changes in the ambient environment should help clients see themselves as "Origins."

Below we would like to discuss some more specific ideas for accomplishing these goals by controlling three important aspects of the ambient environment: indoor climate, sound, and lighting.

Indoor Climate

There are a variety of conventional and alternative energy sources and systems for heating and cooling the home. In reviewing the technology for options, remember to consider the quantity and quality of available controls. Dials, levers, buttons, etc. that are easy to understand and manipulate, and provide for a variety of settings, enhance our feeling of control over the environment.

However, we shouldn't ignore the pretechnological techniques involving both design and structure. These methods not only conserve energy, but also seem to foster a special relationship between people and their surroundings, as the following recollections of an earlier time suggest:

> *The apartment building I lived in as a child was fortress-like, consisting of five solidly built brick wings, six stories high. The brick was insulating. The tar roofs became unbearably hot and sticky to walk on in summer. However, a sprinkler system was activated, which cooled the surface and created a wonderful playground for children in bathing suits. In the evening adults brought lawn chairs and visited with each other under the stars.*

Every summer, awnings which could be manipulated by the tenants were installed outside windows that got sun. We all knew how to keep certain windows closed and others open to get the breeze. Carpets were rolled up and stored in "tar" paper in the corner of a room. I still remember the aroma. Slip covers were cotton and put over all upholstery. The lobbies were terrazzo and bare of carpets in summer. One could always cool off there and socialize with other tenants while using furniture provided by management. I don't remember being miserable without air conditioning in those days.

Perhaps there is a lesson to be learned from remembrances such as these. The simple act of drawing draperies, sliding panels, lowering blinds, and rolling up rugs may give us a greater sense of personal control than operating the ultimate in "high" technology: a programmable, computer-controlled indoor climate system. Although programming a computer may, in fact, give some people a feeling of power over the environment, so that their sense of personal control is augmented, others may react in quite a different manner. They may feel that they are not the ones who are responsible for the effects being produced—it's the machine.

With the old ways, there is no complicated machine to intervene between the person and the environment. Instead, the environment is directly manipulated so that people can more easily experience the pleasure of being a cause.

Of course, we are not advocating a return to the past. But we are suggesting that some of the older techniques are still viable, including the use of fabrics, colors, insulation, and structural materials to create either coolness or warmth. Furthermore, we should not forget that there is a simpler way to use current technology to build upon these earlier techniques and still maintain a direct, harmonious relationship between the person and the environment. Some examples include thermal glass, an upholstered wall system (for instance, a fabric stretched over a frame that is attached to the wall), fabrics manufactured with thermal properties, and vertical blinds, etc.

As you can probably infer from our discussion, people differ with respect to their attitude toward technology and the extent to which they wish to modify the environment technologically to suit their needs. The information obtained from the client interview can be used, with probe questions if necessary, in order to assess these attitudes. Then, appropriate design decisions can be made regarding the use of high technology, low technology, and the earlier climate control techniques.

Sound

Berman (1980) argues that designers should be able to do some acoustical planning in order to heighten music appreciation and provide for sound comfort in the home. Some ideas are also presented in his article to accomplish this goal. For example, for ideal listening in any room there should be a balance between the amount of sound absorbed by soft, porous materials (for example, upholstered furniture, and thick carpeting) and the amount of sound reflected by hard, dense surfaces (for example, walls, mirrors, and hard floors).

Berman also discusses some of the imaginative acoustical strategies employed by Thomas Stanton Gould, ASID, for clients who prefer either a minimalist interior or one that is dominated by soft, absorptive design elements. In the latter situation, speakers can be aimed at the ceiling, or little trap doors can be placed a few feet in front of the speakers to act as reflective surfaces. This idea is particularly interesting to us because clients can easily be shown how to position speakers and "bounce boards" for best listening. Thus, they will have a response that they can perform to increase the quality of the acoustic environment and their sense of personal control as well.

We have had an occasion to use a different approach in a kitchen dominated by hard reflective surfaces. In this case, disturbing reverberations, echoes of voices, and the clanking of utensils bouncing off stucco, wood, and tile surfaces created a din of noise when the space was in use. The clients resisted changing the aesthetic properties of the room, so we employed a compensatory strategy using lighting and plants as distractors. Plants were placed in corners, were hung from the ceiling, and cascaded down the sides of cabinets. We used uplighting, downlighting, and accent lighting to create soft shadows. The family was encouraged to use candlelight for the evening meal in the dining area of the kitchen. And we also selected, with the client, an assortment of visually pleasing, colorful accessories (for instance, a wall hanging and seat cushions for the pine dining chairs).

The approach was quite successful as the problem disappeared within a day or two. In a symbolic sense, the softness of the foliage, candlelight, and shadows counteracted the hardness of the environment, so that the clients were no longer aware of the acoustical problem. And, most importantly, the clients' feelings of personal control were restored when the kitchen was used in the evening for social interaction.

Up to this point, we have been discussing ideas for increasing the acoustical efficiency of the home. Noise problems, sound deadening and sound proofing techniques, etc. will be treated primarily in the next chapter on privacy (see Chapter 3: Control of Information about the Self/Acoustic Output and Interference with Activities/Noise). However, we would like to discuss one such device now because of its relevance to the need for control.

A white noise machine can effectively mask unwanted sound emanating from sources both inside and outside the home. Although the goal of achieving acoustic privacy is an important one, we would like to emphasize that the variety of controls and settings offered by these machines also contributes greatly to a person's sense of control over the acoustic environment by permitting variation in sound quantity, quality, and pattern. The following person's description of one such machine illustrates this point nicely:

> I purchased a white noise machine, and it works well. I can control it in a number of ways. I use it to create a feeling that I am cut off and essentially alone in my house. I also have it on while I am working. It screens me from noise coming through the door; but, essentially, I find that when I switch it on, I am switching on the feeling that I have control over the noise. There are a number of dials: one is for volume, one for treble or bass, one for settings called white sound, surf I, surf II, rain, and waterfall, and two others to control surf rate and surf range. It gives me a great sense of control to adjust them even though the changes are slight. I have used the surf for relaxation and visually was able to see the ocean, based on former memories. I have even heard gulls, which may or may not be built in to the electronic system as squeaks.

Lighting

We have previously listed lighting as one of a number of alternative ways of defining territories. Here we are concerned with the ability to manipulate light and produce various effects in the visual environment. It is beyond the scope of this book to review the many recent advances in the rapidly expanding field of lighting technology with respect to both design and application. Instead, we would simply like to point out some of the different forms of control that are available through lighting so that this technology can be evaluated "in light of" the need for control.

Intensity control

The fact that an ordinary light switch has only two positions—on and off—limits our ability to control light intensity. Light is either present or absent. However, the use of dimmers allows us to have control over the precise amount of light needed for various activities.

The technology may be familiar, but its utility shouldn't be underestimated. An enhanced sense of personal control over the environment results from making these fine adjustments in the level of illumination of a space.

Directional control

Devices that allow us to position a light source appropriately (for example, tracks in various configurations, fixtures that pivot or swivel, and luminaires that hang from adjustable pendants or chains) and direct a light beam into a specific area (for example, low voltage lamps and framing projectors) have obvious advantages for control in relation to more static and less flexible arrangements. Again the idea is to give people a variety of responses to perform for specific purposes such as task lighting, accent lighting, uplighting, downlighting, etc.

Locational control

The placement of control devices can also provide us with a variety of optional responses. Local control is enhanced by having an ample supply of conveniently located electrical outlets and wall switches. "Touch" lamps, because they are activated by direct contact, make us feel even more responsible for the effects that are produced than more traditionally operated lamps. The possibilities for control can also be increased by installing master control panels, area controllers, and portable consoles, which can either be preprogrammed or operated manually to permit multiple location control over lights and other electrical devices.

Outcome control

It is reasonable to assume that our feelings of control are proportional to the variety of visual effects that we can produce. Therefore, we should value those lighting techniques that permit us to simulate various natural conditions (for example, sunrise and sunset), vary patterns of light and shadow, accent forms and textures, etc.

Furnishings

Clients should have the freedom to manipulate the tangible aspects of the environment in addition to the ability to control ambient factors. Therefore, furnishings should be selected to maximize the possibility for change, and the relationship between design elements should be such that the inevitable client re-arrangements do not interfere with room aesthetics and room function.

Soft Architecture

Sommer (1974) advocates a "soft architecture" approach to the design of both indoor and outdoor public spaces such as hospitals, schools, office buildings, airports, and parks. Basically, soft architecture involves the use of building materials, furnishings, and accessories that are soft, comfortable, portable, and flexible.

The changes made to a college classroom by Sommer and Olsen (1980) provide a good example of the application of their approach to the design of public interior space. In the "soft classroom," wooden benches with foam rubber cushions replaced the typical hard student desks. A multicolored carpet was added. Lighting could be adjusted with a rheostat; and decorative items, such as mobiles and wooden paneling, were introduced. Following these renovations, student ratings of the classroom increased dramatically.

Of course, residential interiors are usually furnished with soft, comfortable, and decorative items. It is the public environment that typically needs softening and humanizing—not the home. Instead we wish to emphasize the following additional characteristics of soft architecture, which encourage change, experimentation, and active involvement and, therefore, contribute to a sense of personal control over the home environment.

   1. Adjustability: chairs, tables, beds, shelving units, etc. whose position can be easily changed (for instance, raised, lowered, and tilted) to accommodate the human body. Most of the advances in that branch of human factors concerned with creating designs to fit our physical dimensions and capabilities (for instance, anthropometrics) have been applied to the design of furnishings for the work space. Industrial designers should be encouraged to develop similar adjustable products that are suitable for the residence in style and substance. In the meantime, we can take advantage of whatever limited choices are available, or modify them accordingly. For example, the seating depth of a chair that provides a comfortable fit for a tall person can be decreased with the addition of back pillows to suit a shorter person. Some office furnishings may also be adapted for use in the home (for example, an adjustable office chair, in the appropriate fabrics, as seating for a home work space, a dining room, a kitchen, or a television viewing area). Of course, we need not necessarily be concerned with having a single furnishing fit all people because, unlike the office setting, there are a small number of individuals who occupy a home. Therefore, individualized chairs can be selected to fit the physical requirements of each member of the household as is typically done. Of course, such a solution does not take into account the inevitable physical, biological, and psychological changes that occur in the person over time—changes which may alter preferences and design requirements. Flexible furnishings are, by definition, more responsive to these changes.

   2. Portability: things that can be easily moved from place to place (for example, furniture on castors, lightweight furniture, foldaway tables, port-o-cribs, ottomans, area rugs, pillows, lap desks, and trays).

   3. Multifunctionality: furnishings that have a variety of uses (for example, modular furniture; couches and beds with built-in storage capabilities; sofa beds; cubes used as pedestals for sculpture, surfaces for writing, or as storage for magazines; console tables that open to become dining tables; flip-down surfaces used as tabletops, desks, or bars and platforms for reclining, sleeping, sitting, or eating (Crane, 1982).

Underdesigned Space

   As we looked over our interview data we came across two general descriptions of rooms that provide differential opportunities to exercise environmental control. The first room type, which we will call "over-designed," contains beautiful things arranged in an orderly manner but is also described as being "almost too nice"—a "museum-like" setting that is controlling of people. It communicates the following environmental message to people who enter it:

> Aren't I beautiful. Look at me and appreciate my splendor, but don't touch anything! Don't move anything. Don't change anything. Maybe it would be better if you didn't do anything. Everything is perfect the way it is.

An overdesigned room is overdone, with too much structure and too little room for people to innovate. It is meant to be appreciated at a distance, as a work of art, rather than to be used and manipulated by people to suit their changing needs and preferences. In fact, the furnishings in such a room cannot be re-arranged without partially destroying their intended function and completely destroying the design aesthetics. Overdesigned space seems to create a stagelike environment, with residents moving about the "set" like actors rather than living in the home like real people. Although the space may have aesthetic appeal to some and may be relevant to the need for order (see Chapter 6: Perceptual Organization/Balance), it is certainly not well suited for a client with a strong control need.

On the other hand, the second type of room, which we will call "underdesigned," is described variously as comfortable, functional, flexible, and lived in—and, thus, is more open to personal control. It seems to be saying the following:

> Be comfortable. I am here for you, so change me around whenever you want. You are in control here.

Now that we have defined the concepts of overdesigned and underdesigned space in a general sense, let's discuss some more specific differences between them.

1. In overdesigned areas, one often finds balanced compositions in which the interrelationship among elements precludes the removal of any one of them—or else the symmetry would be thrown off (for example, an Oriental painting/sconce combination flanking each side of a window and a pair of very low teakwood chests beneath the window—creating a composition with the window view acting as a landscape mural of trees). In an underdesigned room, paintings, photographs, and other wall-hung objects could be substituted in order to provide more flexible and interchangeable arrangements that still can be aesthetically balanced.

2. Some overdesigned rooms contain complex backgrounds (for example, patterned wallpaper with matching draw draperies) that prohibit wall displays because of the conflicting and confusing patterns that would result. Alternatively, simple backgrounds (for example, solid-painted or solid-covered walls) could be used, so that occupants would be free to display pictures, collections, etc.

3. Overdesigned space gives the appearance of being finished and complete. Even the open spaces appear to be filled, or at least it is obvious that they should not be filled in. On the other hand, an underdesigned room may contain an unfinished corner—a place that occupants could experiment with, change, and transform. Sometimes a certain degree of incompleteness is desirable, so that people are encouraged to fill in the gaps and project their own personalities onto the space.

4. An overdesigned area may contain elements whose form, size, and function fixes their location (for example, a coffee table, or a dining table), whereas an underdesigned area contains elements that can function in a variety of locations without disturbing the aesthetics (for example, a nest of tables or a table with drop leaves).

In summary, we are suggesting that furnishings be put together using the essential elements of design (for example, form, texture, color, scale, line, and mass), as well as the ideas presented in this section, to create underdesigned areas that are capable of undergoing numerous transformations without disturbing their aesthetic and functional integrity. Instead of thinking in terms of fixed, static, uni-dimensional spaces that reinforce the observer role of the individual and, thus, artificially separate people from their surroundings, we should be designing living spaces that welcome the individual as an integral part of the environment. Aesthetic principles need not be compromised by this strategy; however, a somewhat different, and more flexible, theory of beauty must be adopted (see Chapter 8: Distance versus Engagement).

Activities

Designers can help their clients appropriate and furnish areas within the home to pursue hobbies and interests and perfect skills. Personal control is enhanced by the opportunity to engage in such activities for people of all ages, but the benefits may be particularly important for those who may see themselves as being low in competence (for example, the elderly, the disabled, and the young).

For example, Langer and Rodin (1976) found that residents of a nursing home who were given plants to care for had a greater sense of well-being than a similar group of residents who were offered plants that were cared for by the nursing home staff. A sense of personal control is fostered by the very act of operating upon the environment—by watering, feeding, transplanting, etc.—and by seeing that our efforts result in some tangible benefit (for instance, the growth of flowers and vegetables).

Some of these psychological benefits of gardening can be experienced in the home environment using sunlight from windows, greenhouses, and other indoor arrangements (R. Kaplan, 1973); or other activity areas that give people a chance to manipulate, alter, and experiment with objects in the environment can be designed to fit the interests and abilities of the client.

The activity-area concept seems to be particularly well suited for children. Parents should be sensitive to their children's interests, provide the space to pursue them, offer financial support for any necessary equipment and/or encouragement for earning their own money, and adopt a hands-off policy after that. In this manner, children are given the opportunity to develop self-control, responsibility, competence, and a respect for the rights and property of others, as the following personal account illustrates:

> *My daughter worked at little jobs when she was old enough (at the riding stable and babysitting in the neighborhood) to earn money to buy camera equipment, which included an expensive telephoto lens to photograph the race horses in action at Saratoga. We provided her, or rather allowed her, to do what she wanted with the space she selected. She turned the pump-water-tank room in the basement into a dark room for photo processing. She also used the kitchen because she needed water and there is no sink downstairs. Although it was initially a nuisance to me, with cooperation regarding hours we got along with it. Because our house is so small, the activities she pursued (music, recording, art, and so on) sometimes took up corners of shared spaces. But because we were considerate of her need to do so, she was considerate of our needs for her not to be obtrusive. Now she has a very strong identity of her own and seems to be very happy as a person.*

Although there will certainly be a wide variety of individual differences in interests among children, there are two specific ideas for activity areas that we think would have broad appeal: a science center and an indoor adventure playground.

Children enjoy learning about the environment, and manipulating it, by doing "experiments" in the sciences (for example, chemistry, physics, astronomy, and biology). We can reinforce this natural scientific curiosity by designing space for children to have the kinds of experiences that the following people recalled with fondness:

I tried to collect caterpillars, put them in milk bottles, feed them leaves, and induce them to metamorphose into butterflies, with no success whatsoever.

My brother loved to do experiments with his chemistry set. A variety of odors would emanate from the cellar, where he used to mix his chemicals. Every once in a while there would be a mild explosion, which would upset our mother, but no harm was ever done. Later he got a degree in chemistry and is now working as an engineer.

Our interviews also revealed a second common manipulative strategy. Children love to engage in creative play, using whatever materials are available (for example, pillows, chairs, and blankets), to build tunnels, form enclosures, etc.

Note the following childhood recollections:

Bookcases were built into the walls of my room. I remember playing Barbie dolls and using these shelves as their house.

I loved to build houses with large cushions ransacked from the sun porch.

As a child I spent many hours in my living room playing with dolls. I would build houses out of album covers and make furniture with whatever I could find.

Many times children will attempt to re-arrange furniture to build their play structures. Parents may tolerate this behavior for a while but quickly ask their children to put things back where they belong and use these objects the way they were intended to be used. It would be much better to reinforce the child's tendency to control the environment—rather than limit it—by giving the child a space furnished with objects that can be put together, taken apart, transformed, and used in many different ways. It would also be advantageous for the space to have various structural irregularities (for example, alcoves, slanted ceilings, and levels), which could be easily incorporated into the child's play experience.

Such a place would resemble the outdoor adventure playground, in which natural materials are used by children to build swings, jungle gyms, and other play objects and spaces. A further discussion of the function and the design of children's play areas is presented in Chapter 3: Social Withdrawal/Places for Emotional Release.

PRIVACY

— 3 —

People are generally able to verbalize their concerns about privacy quite easily. They say things like the following:

I'm a very private person so I need my own space.

I got a lock for my room so I would have more privacy.

I have a great need for privacy.

I am a solitary individual.

However, privacy does not have a simple meaning; it takes on many forms, and is expressed in different ways. Therefore, we will discuss four different dimensions of privacy (for instance, control of information about the self, interference with activities, social withdrawal, and privacy regulation) and provide design concepts that are appropriate for satisfying each of these varieties of the need.

Control of Information About the Self

Margulis (1979) sees privacy as a process of information management. At times, people wish to withhold personal information in order to avoid being stereotyped, ridiculed, punished, or controlled by others. Usually, people verbalize this tendency by expressing a desire that their behavior be unknown to others:

I used to turn down the lights so no one could tell what I was doing.

We used to sit in front of the stereo and listen to music. This location gave us privacy because if there was anyone in the next room, they couldn't see us from there.

It would also be important to keep in mind that this need is not limited to adults. It appears in early adolescence and is emphasized particularly by children who share a room (Wolfe and Laufer, 1975).

Visual Output

Under certain circumstances people wish to maintain visual privacy; that is, they do not wish to be seen. Thus, one of our subjects said:

I like to lay on the floor with a pillow and watch TV in my family room. Sometimes, people come over in the early evening to see my wife or children. I get embarrassed for them to see me laying on the floor, particularly if I'm in my pajamas.

The design concepts to follow may be used if this visual privacy theme is mentioned in client interviews.

Visual barriers

Some of the territorial boundary techniques listed in the previous chapter on control can also be used to prevent visual information about a person from reaching others in the same space. Visual barriers can be created by using objects, furniture, screens, panels, partitions, etc.

For example, a person could be concealed from view while sitting in a high, fan-back wicker chair surrounded by plants, hanging baskets, and some sculpture. This gardenlike setting could be located in a screened porch, attached greenhouse, or in the corners of shared rooms. In this application, a combination of furniture and other objects helps us achieve a feeling of being inconspicuous.

Because no one can see what we are doing, we can feel very comfortable doing whatever we want at the moment—writing a private letter, reading, or just dozing off. Of course, other styles, arrangements, and locations are possible (for example, an eighteenth-century wing-back chair used in a multi-purpose room or bedroom, or a high-back executive desk chair in a home office or den), depending upon the specific visual privacy needs of the client.

Partitioning can be used effectively in a number of different contexts. A lady may prefer to have a screen around her dressing table so that grooming can be accomplished in private. As the noted sociologist Erving Goffman (1959) has argued, people need time to be "off-stage," relax, and get ready for later "public performances." At such a time, people may prefer not to be observed. Thus, the lady is able to preserve some of the magic and mystery of life in her screened-off, backstage dressing area.

One person mentioned that he likes to do stretching exercises in the bedroom soon after awakening in the morning. However, he feels self-conscious with his body stretched out in various positions on the floor if others happen to be using the room at the same time. In this case, sliding panels on tracks could be used to produce a temporary, but visually protected, exercise area.

As we mentioned before, the visual privacy needs of children and adolescents should not be ignored. Thus, in consultation with the parents, designers can give children the flexibility to create a variety of visually protected spaces as needed with modular storage units, cubes, shades, curtains, etc.

Other applications of the partitioning approach include structural partitioning of convenience equipment in a shared bath, and draperies or Shoji panels surrounding the bed.

These visual barrier suggestions are doubly useful as both privacy and control needs can be simultaneously satisfied. Panels can be slid into place; draperies can be drawn; curtains can be pulled. In this way, we are able to manipulate the environment (for example, experience personal control) in order to achieve privacy. In fact, these two needs are very closely related. One probably cannot have privacy without some degree of environmental control.

Up until now we have been talking about achieving visual privacy from others who are within the dwelling. Additionally, people are concerned with being seen from the outside through windows. However, the design problem is somewhat complicated by the fact that a view is also highly desirable.

Hill (1970) performed a very interesting "optimization experiment" in which people were asked to choose the best mesh material for curtains in two different rooms (for instance, the bedroom and the kitchen) with either a landscape view or a view of a pedestrian walkway. Using Hill's terminology, net curtains can differ in optical transmission through changes in thread thickness, weave orientation, weave density, etc. In this experiment, people chose from among six different solid-to-void ratios of the weave.

Some of Hill's results may be helpful in making decisions about appropriate window treatments for the client. In private areas of the home (for example, bedroom and bath), the need to avoid visual exposure predominates (for instance, people chose very high solid-to-void ratios). The exposure problem is particularly critical if the window happens to overlook a public area. However, in bedrooms overlooking open areas, people are willing to sacrifice some visual privacy to take advantage of the view.

For example, one person mentioned to us that his bedroom window overlooks a nearby woodsy area. Because it is rare for anyone to be there outside (for instance, the potential for visual exposure is low), the window is left uncovered. He can even dress there comfortably without worrying about being seen and can have the feeling of being in a natural setting during the process.

Similarly, outside visual privacy is less of a problem in public areas of the home. Thus, in kitchens, Hill's subjects chose relatively low solid-to-void ratios, particularly in combination with a landscape-type view.

As you can see, a number of factors have to be considered for each individual case when making decisions concerning fenestration. What is the function of the room? What will occupants be doing there? Will people require visual privacy while they engage in these behaviors? Does the window overlook public or private areas? Is it likely that people will be in these outside areas in position to view indoor activities? What are the client's individual preferences for privacy versus views?

After these questions are answered, an informed design decision can be made for a particular person in a particular room location. Of course, a variety of solutions are possible besides variation of weave density in a net curtain. Other types of screening materials can be used: blinds, draperies, etc., which can be opened or closed at different times of the day. Or, one-way viewing can be accomplished (for instance, you can see out, but others can't see in) with one-way materials (for example, glass and shades), mirror arrangements, or high sills.

Instead of treating the inside of a window, a structural partition can be used. on the outside of a ground-floor window. The partition should be placed some distance away from the window to allow for air circulation and to prevent a closed-in feeling. It can be attached to the house or be free standing. In order to compensate for the loss of a view, an attractive "scene" can be created by using decorative, visually pleasing material for the wall, landscaping, or other more creative solutions.

Orientation

Generally speaking, furnishings can be oriented in such a manner as to make it difficult for people to observe one another's behavior.

For example, the high-back chair, mentioned earlier, would have its back to traffic areas. Face-to-face seating arrangements are employed in living rooms, multi-purpose areas, etc. to encourage conversation. The message that such a room sends to its occupants is clear: "When you're here, you're supposed to interact with other people." However, back-to-back seating allows each person to engage in solitary behavior without being observed. The message communicated by this arrangement is quite different:

> The people who sit here want visual privacy. You may do whatever you want on an individual basis, but pay attention to your own behavior, and don't look at what other people are doing.

If one does not wish to communicate such a severe message of distance between people, smaller angles of orientation (for instance, between 90° and 180°) can be used to reduce visual exposure in a more subtle manner. Or, partial visual barriers can be combined with slight orientation differences to produce the same effect.

Lighting

Lamps could be dimmed to such a level that no one would be able to see what others are doing. That wouldn't be very practical because people wouldn't be able to see what they were doing either. But, it may be possible to use focused lighting, in combination with barriers and orientation techniques, to provide sufficient light for one's activities and protect visual privacy as well. Perhaps we can look to theatrical lighting for inspiration. One such theatrical technique is to illuminate the surface of an otherwise ineffective visual barrier, rendering the individual invisible behind a protective shield of light.

Room shape

Various room configurations can block lines of sight, thereby producing some degree of visual protection for individuals desiring privacy. We can take advantage of existing deviations from rectilinearity (for example, L-shapes and cloverleaves), which naturally result in pockets of low visual exposure. Alternatively, rooms can be structurally altered with built-ins, diagonals, walls, etc. For example, a plywood or fiberglass structure with a bench, built into a protected corner of a room, can function as a privacy alcove.

Acoustic Output

People also would like to have acoustic privacy. In other words, there are times at which they do not wish to be heard by others. A most interesting illustration of this point is provided by the following account:

> I get carried away when I'm watching football games at home on the TV. I'm always screaming, shouting and cheering, but I feel kind of inhibited when I know that other people can hear me. So I go down to the cellar, but I still don't get the privacy I need.

The design concepts to follow can be used to help the client cope with the variety of contexts in which acoustic privacy is a primary concern.

Sound-absorbing materials

The use of soft, porous materials on walls, windows, floors, ceilings, and furnishings can deaden sound within a space. Some examples include: well-padded, high-pile, wall-to-wall carpeting, attractive fabric wall hangings on canvas stretchers, window panels or shutters with fabric inserts, ceiling tiles made of acoustic fabric, and fully upholstered seating. Speaking softly, people may be able to carry on private conversations in the corner of a fairly large room treated in this manner.

However, there are problems with a room that contains a high ratio of absorbing to reflecting materials. Overall acoustics would be poor, making it difficult to use that space for social purposes or for listening to music. The soft architectural style may not suit everyone. And, more importantly for privacy, people may require a greater degree of acoustic isolation from others. Of course, sound absorption may be combined with some of the following techniques to provide additional acoustic protection.

Booths and enclosures

Instead of attempting to acoustically treat the entire room, a "privacy booth" can be designed in a limited area of a room (for example, with false walls of acoustic panels on tracks or pivots, plywood enclosures covered with sound-absorbing materials built into, or out of, a wall, etc.). Such an area could function quite nicely as a telephone booth.

There are times when people would prefer that other household members not overhear their telephone conversations. It's not so much that people are communicating secret information; it's more of a question of being able to say what you want, in any way that you want, without feeling self-conscious. Or, one may simply wish to share an intimate thought or feeling with a loved one, so that it wouldn't be appropriate for others (for example, visitors and children) to be within earshot.

If used for telephone conversations, the booth should be centrally located so as to be accessible to all members of the household. It should also be well ventilated and could be quite imaginatively decorated.

The enclosure concept can also be used effectively in more private areas of the home where walls do not completely screen out potentially embarrassing noises that people make when engaging in private bathroom and bedroom behaviors. More specifically, the toilet area can be enclosed and sound-deadened, and the bed can be acoustically shielded by using fabric canopies, built-in alcoves, or sliding panels. Then, people may be able to engage in private activities freely without being inhibited by the knowledge that others know, and can hear, what they are doing.

Selection and modification of equipment for quiet operation

Noise from equipment, which calls attention to the occurrence of intimate activities, can be further reduced by some of the following techniques:

1. Fiberglass collars and a swing arm to allow movement to eliminate noise from expanding hot water lines.

2. Holes for pipes sealed, and air leaks plugged.

3. Toilets with quiet flushing and refilling cycles.

4. Soft toilet seats or carpeted commode lids to prevent clatter.

5. Plastic, instead of glass or ceramic, toilet articles and storage holders, securely installed.

6. Hardware, including hinges on doors and cabinets, that operates quietly.

7. Bedding with well-made inner springs held securely in a sturdy frame.

8. A bed built into a sound-insulated platform.

Sound isolation through structure

Special circumstances may exist that require the effective soundproofing of a room or rooms. A musician may desire a rehearsal room; a business person, politician, or student may need a place to practice speeches and presentations. Generally speaking, when people are in the act of creating, they try out new techniques, make errors, and would, therefore, prefer not to be heard until they are at their best.

There are also situations that go beyond mere embarrassment. It may be threatening to people for others to have access to certain information. For example, sensitive business discussions may take place in the home. Personal problems may be aired. Furthermore, the situation may be exacerbated by the fact that common walls are shared with neighbors in apartments, townhomes, etc.

In these cases, sound should be controlled with structure; and, if necessary, an acoustical engineer may be consulted. Generally speaking, effective room soundproofing requires double, but separate walls, with the air space between filled with insulating materials. Berman's (1980) article in *Residential Interiors* presents some of the recommendations of Thomas Stanton Gould, ASID, in this regard.

If the client's living circumstances do not permit the structural modification of walls, storage units or bookcases can be placed along walls that transmit sound to others in adjoining rooms. If possible an air space should be left between the unit and the wall. In this case, the floor must be absolutely level, and the aesthetic problem of viewing the space behind the unit must be overcome. If the unit contains cabinets, additional acoustic protection can be provided by backing the doors or panels with insulation.

The air-space idea can also be applied in the vertical dimension by dropping a new ceiling. Standard acoustic tiles may not be appropriate for this purpose because of aesthetic considerations. Instead, a decorative effect can be achieved with colorful fabric tiles or panels used in combination with attractive grids of brass or polished steel.

Alternatively, an open frame can be dropped from the ceiling. Panels of stained glass, colored film, gels, or plastic—interspersed with hanging plants—can be installed along with concealed or decorative lighting. The ceiling could also be divided into sections to aid in the definition of individual territories within the room.

This design would result in a beautiful natural setting, absorbing sound. Additionally, acoustical tiles, hidden by the suspended ceiling, could be installed on the real ceiling without creating an aesthetic problem.

Of course, sufficient head room should be available. Some people experience an uncomfortable feeling of enclosure in rooms with low ceilings. However, others might actually enjoy having their heads brushed by hanging plants as they grow. Therefore, it is important to take into account individual differences in client preferences for such things as ceiling height, contact with nature, and panel materials.

Masking

All of the preceding techniques attempt to block the transmission of sound in some manner. Alternatively, noise, conversation, etc. can be rendered unintelligible to others through masking.

Mandatory vent fans installed in bathrooms without windows are typically switched on, not for ventilation, but for masking bathroom noises. We could facilitate this masking process by using white noise machines in bathrooms, bedrooms, dens, etc. Or, we could use more interesting and pleasing masking sounds (for example, music), which also would improve the aesthetic quality of the acoustic environment.

Tapes could be activated during bathroom use. Of course, if the music is turned on only when acoustic privacy is desired, a clear signal is sent to others that private activities are taking place. Then, privacy may still be violated even though sound is effectively masked. People wouldn't know what we were doing, but they would know that we were doing it. Therefore, it would be better to instruct people to activate the tape each time the room is used, whether for private activities or not, or have the tape come on automatically. In this way, an association would not necessarily be formed between the music, the use of the room, and the occurrence of private behavior.

Interference with Activities

For many people, having privacy means avoiding intrusions, interruptions, and distractions so that desired activities can be completed without interference from others.

This form of privacy was mentioned quite often by our subjects:

It is almost a necessity that I have a room where I will not be disturbed.

The most significant room to me was my bedroom. I didn't like it to be intruded upon by anybody.

I need a place that I can study in without distraction.

Interference problems are often magnified when guests or relatives move into the home on a temporary or a permanent basis: "When one of my grandparents moved in with us, I made a room down in our basement where I could do my work or read."

It seems that the first thing people think of in avoiding interference is to have separate spaces, as indicated by the preceding "stories." And, in fact, total isolation may be required for activities that involve concentrated effort over an extended time period. Many of the techniques that are described in this section offer less extreme solutions, which can be applied selectively to eliminate particular distractors. These concepts can also be combined with each other to produce varying degrees of protection from interference. And, they are flexible enough to be used in both shared spaces and separate rooms.

Visual Distractions

There are several contexts in which people may be distracted by the presence of changing visual stimuli in the environment, particularly the sight of other people: when they are working on important tasks that require concentration and when they are immersed in enjoyable leisure activities like reading. In these cases, some of the techniques that we described for preventing people from being seen (for instance, control of visual output) can be used just as well for preventing people from seeing others (for instance, control of visual input).

These methods include the following: partial or complete visual barriers, orientation of seating away from areas of activity, differential lighting of a room with potential distractors located in areas of low illumination, and room shapes that block lines of sight.

Noise

Sounds made by other people, objects, or machines are usually perceived as noise when our concentration is disturbed by them. If we were not otherwise occupied with personally important activities, these same sounds might be interpreted in a positive manner. Thus, the perception of noise is rather subjective, depending upon our current tasks and goals.

Again, you should be guided by our discussion of methods for controlling acoustic output. Thus, sound absorption, quiet equipment, structural isolation, and masking can be used to control incoming noise as well. We would, however, like to make some additions and elaborations that are particularly appropriate to the problem of controlling acoustic input.

In many homes, people use kitchen or dining room tables as work surfaces. Other spatial arrangements (for example, first-floor dens, multi-purpose areas, and family rooms) also result in the location of work and play activities in close proximity to the kitchen. Kitchen noise may, then, create a potential privacy problem by interfering with these behaviors. The following constitutes a partial list of techniques which can be used to solve this problem:

1. Quiet kitchen floors (for example, carpeting, area rugs, and cork combined with vinyl).

2. Insulation of appliances.

3. Small appliances mounted on springs or pads, large appliances leveled, range hoods and food-waste disposers, etc. properly installed—all to minimize vibration.

4. Removable plastic racks to eliminate the clatter of dishes, glasses, and utensils.

5. Thick rubber mats, stored for use on counter tops and other surfaces.

6. Ballasts with rubber mounts to minimize the hum of fluorescent lights.

7. Fully upholstered seats.

8. Wood cabinets, rather than metal ones, to reduce the reflection of sound.

9. Fabric insulation lining the inside of cabinet doors, or a frame with padded or quilted fabric inserts installed on the outside.

10. Movable, sound-absorbing partitions, dividing the kitchen area from adjacent work and play areas, in order to provide some acoustic protection when both areas are in use.

We would also like to discuss some additional applications of the masking strategy. In New York City, waterfalls have been used in small parks to mask urban noise (Holahan, 1982). Attractive indoor fountains, combined with sculpture, foliage, etc., could perform a similar function, providing acoustic protection from both indoor and outdoor noise. A person could, then, use the fountain area for activities requiring acoustic privacy and have the additional advantage of being surrounded by beauty.

Some thought should be given to the proper location of the fountain. For example, it may be used in an area with an outside noise problem (for example, a room facing a heavily trafficked street). Perhaps the fountain should not be located where it might interfere with communication among dwelling members although it could be activated only when needed for privacy. Additionally, it would be important for the fountain to be designed so that water is recycled to avoid waste.

Finally, devices such as earphones and headphones can be used for selective listening to radios, stereos, and television sets. In this way, the listener is protected from extraneous noise. At the same time, others are similarly not disturbed.

Behavioral Planning

It may be helpful to use a variant of Ittelson, Rivlin, and Proshansky's (1970) behavioral mapping technique as a part of the client interview, in order to locate potential areas of conflict and interference. Simply ask the client to indicate on a map of the home interior where various activities are performed by different family members.

In analyzing the map, look for mutually interfering activities that are performed in adjacent areas. Different spatial arrangements can, then, be suggested in order to separate these behaviors.

For example, in one individual's home, the phone was located in the family room very close to the heavily watched television set. With this arrangement, it was difficult for both activities to take place simultaneously without violating the privacy of each party. Several years later, the phone was moved to a desk in an adjacent room. Then, the separation between activities was great enough to prevent interference, but not so great as to isolate family members from each other.

Bechtel (1977) describes similar "boundary problems" that occur in work settings such as offices and hospitals. Even though the places he discusses are quite different, it still may be possible to apply some of his solutions to the residential environment.

Incompatible behaviors can also be separated in another way, by making use of areas over which a person has control. In other words, certain activities can be located inside an individual's personal territory.

One of our subjects expressed such a desire to use territoriality as a way of minimizing intrusion in the morning thusly: "I would like to be able to eat my breakfast and read the paper in my bedroom."

Behavioral maps may also reveal potential traffic problems within the home. Traffic patterns can, then, be altered with fixed or movable partitions to produce protected areas for privacy.

This solution would have been helpful to one member of our sample who "likes to watch TV, watch the fire, talk and read" on the couch in her den. However, these activities were often interrupted by the kids, who "use the den as a traffic area to get from the front to the back of the house." Partitions, protecting the open entrances to the den, would increase the usage of an underused hallway route, which also connects front and back regions of the house.

Signs, Signals, and Symbols

The design concepts discussed to this point all have one thing in common: Behavioral interference is reduced by some form of physical restraint. In other words, the transmission of distracting stimuli is blocked, and people are physically separated from each other. Alternatively, the environment can be used as a medium of communication, signaling to others that a person does not wish to be intruded upon. Of course, in order for this approach to work properly, there must be the kind of mutual respect that one would hope to find among people who are sharing the same dwelling.

In shared areas, territorial boundaries can be symbolically defined, by using any of the techniques described in Chapter 2: partial partitions, objects, shape, lighting, color, pattern, and elevation. These elements send messages of ownership of space to others, increasing the chances that they will respect our privacy rights when we occupy the symbolically bounded area. For example, the accent color, or any other color that is part of the total scheme, can be used to delineate a private area within a shared room.

Instead of having a fixed color, colored light or projected gels can be used to temporarily define a privacy space. This area (or areas) could be the exclusive property of one person or be shared. Then, depending upon whoever is using the area, that person's favorite color can be projected. One person can be blue, another yellow, and so on. Alternatively, neon-tube lighting can border the space and be activated when in use, or area rugs can be unrolled, screens unfolded, etc.

Then, people can avoid the embarrassment of having to say aloud: "I don't want to be with you right now; I have some things to do by myself, and I don't want you to interrupt me." Instead the message can be communicated in a more subtle manner by simply occupying the agreed upon privacy area. This form of nonverbal communication allows people to accomplish their goals without hurting anyone else's feelings.

Areas under the exclusive control of individuals or groups (for example, dens and bedrooms) are less likely to be violated than shared areas of the home. However, when intrusions and interruptions do occur in these places, they are particularly annoying.

Security systems include electronic devices that activate alarms, flashing lights, etc. to warn us about potential intrusions. Of course, we ordinarily wouldn't resort to such drastic solutions in order to protect our privacy from other family members. However, a gentler, and more artistic, method of warning might be considered.

Imagine the following situation. You are working or recreating in your own room. As another household member attempts to enter the room, a beautiful display of light and color is electronically activated. Different colors can be used to signal different degrees of approachability: red—"I'm struggling with a difficult problem; it would be best to stay away now"; blue—"I can be interrupted under certain circumstances; knock and ask permission to enter"; green—"Come on in; I am available."

Sound can replace, or be combined with, visual stimuli, with buzzers and tinkling bells representing opposite points along the mood spectrum. Hums, chimes, taped music, or even verbal messages can be employed as cues, informing others of a person's current level of desired privacy.

Social Withdrawal

In the previous section on interference, we argued that people need at least partial isolation from others in order to accomplish certain tasks. Here we are concerned with social withdrawal for its own sake.

Constant social interaction is demanding and effortful. Sometimes we need a rest, a time that we can experience the self apart from others.

Physical Separation

The availability of spatially separated areas from which to choose certainly enhances our ability to experience aloneness in a positive way. Thus, the design concepts to follow are all directed toward achieving that goal.

Individual territories

In Chapter 2 we argued that it is highly desirable, space permitting, for each member of the household to have a room to own and occupy. One of the advantages of controlling space is that the area can be used for privacy. Then, we know that there is always somewhere to go in order to separate ourselves from others and experience solitude.

Retreats

Retreats carry the idea of private territories one step further. Through various design elaborations, areas such as bedrooms, private baths, etc., can be converted into psychologically secure places of refuge. Surrounded by our own things, the walls become our outer shell, allowing us to go inside ourselves as we enter the room. This feeling of retreating into the self can be further enhanced by interposing another protective layer between us and the outside world. Thus, the environmental enclosures described in Chapter 2, or privacy cubicles of various types, can be located within the larger walled area.

Some years ago, a design student at the Parsons School of Design developed such an idea by creating "a room within a room." A circular structure in the center of the room had shelves for book storage along the outside walls, but could also be entered through an opening. The inside was appropriately furnished to provide a private sanctuary for study, reading, and writing.

The preceding design probably would have worked well for a subject who said: "I use my den as my little retreat; I read books and magazines in here and escape into another world."

The bathroom is another place that could be designed as a retreat, as suggested by the following interview: "I would like to have my very own bathroom, which I would make very luxurious and feminine; it would be my own little retreat."

Yet, Altman and Chemers (1980) correctly point out that although the bathroom is often used to get away from people, its design provides a poor fit for various solitary activities. Comfortable seating is usually absent. Bathrooms lack proper environmental supports for reading (for example, good lighting and book racks). Facilities for having snacks are inadequate. And, generally speaking, the bathroom lacks amenities for the kind of private nurturance of the self that we consider important.

Bedrooms are also used frequently for avoiding others and being alone:

The bedroom would be a retreat from the other goings on in the house, my own private space. Being inside four walls, I tend to block out the world and turn up the volume.

Unfortunately, the bedroom is often the most neglected area in the home. Instead of being regarded as a prime location for solitude, escape, and self-indulgence, it is often relegated to the bottom of the design-budget list. Furnishings are generally stereotyped and bought as a set, and little money is spent there, except in a decorative way (for example, for pretty colors and fabrics). Public areas of the home are given a much higher priority.

And, yet, with a little imagination the bedroom could be transformed into a secret place, safely away from people—a place for the nourishment of the psyche. The bed could be placed on a platform, lit skillfully so that it appears to float, suspended from stable or swinging ropes, changed in shape to be round, oval, or hexagonal, located under a skylight, surrounded with foliage. The bed could be a period piece in a castlelike setting, a bordello in France, etc. The person could be surrounded by a protective sheath of changing colors, climates, and fragrances that can be controlled electronically—whatever the individual desires.

Places for emotional release

According to Westin (1970), one of the functions of solitude is emotional release. People need a respite from the social roles they play. They require temporary relief from the demands of others, and they must have time to relax and be themselves. Therefore, we are suggesting that separate places in the home, for fantasy and games, be set aside for this purpose. For some people singing in the shower is an enjoyable, emotionally releasing activity. This area is chosen because it is private, and hard surfaces create resonant sound. But why not design an enclosed shower specifically for such a person in order to enhance the acoustical environment even further? Thus, proper acoustical planning can create a richness of sound within the area and prevent sound from leaking out of the area as well.

Multi-media rooms, electronic game rooms, and exercise rooms are other examples of environments where adults can entertain themselves and be free of constraining rules, customs, and obligations.

But let us not forget the children. They also need to get away from the social demands of adults—perhaps in a room of play and fantasy with storage space for collections, things that can be put together and taken apart, washable wall surfaces, a platform for a stage, and dress-up clothes. Such an area could be located in a finished basement, a place where parents are more likely to give children the freedom to manipulate things, make noise, and generally act like kids.

Psychological Separation

Due to spatial limitations, it is not always possible to have physically separate spaces to escape from social interaction and be alone. However, shared spaces can be designed to facilitate psychological escape as a substitute for physical withdrawal.

Windows

We will have much to say about windows, in different chapters, because they perform a number of important functions for people. In this context, windows provide an avenue of visual escape for those who have few places to go in order to be by themselves. For example, it would be desirable to have a window included in the territory claimed by each child in a shared bedroom.

The advantages of this arrangement for privacy are illustrated quite nicely by the following account:

*When I lived at home, I shared a very small bedroom with my
brother. My bed was located next to the wall that contained the
only window. On summer evenings, when we were both in the
room, I used to spend a lot of time looking through the window at
the houses and alley below. There wasn't much to see, but I'd
usually get lost in thought after awhile. It was relaxing and the
window allowed me to "escape" from a crowded situation.*

The process of comfortably withdrawing into a private world of
thought can be further reinforced: "My bedroom had a built-in window
seat, with a lovely huge window. . . . I spent much time there reading and
thinking."

If a natural window seat is not present (for example, that provided by a
dormer window), a private sitting area can be designed with benches, etc.
A translucent screen can be used behind the person to further define the
area, provide some visual privacy from others in the room, and still
adequately light the area.

Surrogate views and total environments

Some research has indicated that people need help in detaching themselves from their environment. For example, S. Miller (1981) suggested
that people use imagery to try to distance themselves from others in shared
spaces and, thus, avoid feelings of crowding. However, many subjects reported that their images of distant places were difficult to sustain for two
reasons: It was hard to ignore the close presence of others, and there was
nothing in their immediate environment to reinforce the image.

Although this research was conducted in public environments, we
may still be able to apply the results to the design of shared interior spaces.
As we have argued previously, the presence of a window provides some environmental support for the process of psychological escape or distancing.
But, if no window is available for this purpose, indoor views may be substituted.

*We used to hang large planters from the ceiling. I often felt as if I
were in a tropical rain forest. It was the perfect place to escape,
both physically and mentally.*

This subject's experience suggests several approaches. First of all, indoor gardens may help people enter an imaginary world of solitude. Sec-

ondly, any design techniques that symbolize faraway places may perform the same function.

A view can be created with a mural of wallpaper, paintings, or an enlarged photo printed on canvas to cover the whole wall. The feeling of being surrounded by a "total environment" can be further enhanced by the use of visually compatible sound tapes—of a waterfall, an ocean, or birds chirping in a meadow.

In addition to representing natural settings or distant places, the total environment may simply be a favorite place. We can ask the client to "imagine yourself in a favorite place, a private place, or a place that provides a restful refuge from other people." Then, based upon the client's responses, a simulation of the imagined environment can be created.

Common or alternate foci

If each person in a room were focusing on some common stimulus, attention would be directed toward the environment and away from people. Therefore, shared areas could be furnished with things that people enjoy watching or listening to, so that each individual could achieve a feeling of aloneness.

Television watching provided a common focus for the members of the following family: "I like to watch TV with my family. . . . Since everyone is absorbed in watching the TV, I feel like I'm the only one there."

Alternatively, each person could be involved in a different activity, or view a different environment, with the same result. For example, multipurpose areas could be designed with adjacent, noninterfering activity areas for each occupant.

Of course, these heterogeneous spaces must be designed in such a way as to avoid visual chaos. Similarly, compatible environments can be combined in a shared room (for example, a fireplace and a scenic mural) to provide an involving view for each person.

Privacy Regulation

In the last section, we discussed privacy as being physically and/or psychologically separate from other people. According to Altman (1975), social withdrawal is only one aspect of a more general privacy regulation process. The important point is for people to have the ability to regulate social interaction so that they get the right amount of it to fit their changing privacy needs. Sometimes people want to be with others; sometimes they want to be away from others; and, sometimes they want a little of each. Therefore, the design concepts in this section should help people achieve a balance between accessibility to others and inaccessibility from others.

Functional Separation

The typical American solution to the privacy regulation problem is to have spatially separate facilities for interaction and solitude (Altman, 1975). First-floor family rooms serve as gathering places for family members, whereas second-floor bedrooms and bathrooms are used as places for being alone. Or, social areas are confined to front rooms, and solitary places such as dens and workshops are located in the rear of the home. In order to achieve a desired level of privacy/social contact, people simply go to the appropriate area.

Multifunctional Space

The idea of having each room perform a different function requires a lot of space. However, our cultural legacy of spaciousness may be coming to an end as we must learn to adjust to higher dwelling densities and less usable space per dwelling. Therefore, we may have to adopt solutions similar to the Japanese, who use flexible design elements so that a space may be altered to serve different purposes at different times (Altman, 1975).

In the second chapter, we argued that the use of soft architecture allows people to manipulate their surroundings easily and comfortably. Using this approach, rooms can be furnished in order to function as places for both social interaction and aloneness thusly:

1. Portable furnishings can be moved in and out (for example, floor pillows, a nest of tables, and chairs on castors).

2. Modular furniture can be re-arranged to produce conversational groupings or solitary seating.

3. Convertibles can be used for sleeping or entertaining.

4. Flexible barriers can be put up or taken down. The children's bed-

room described in Chapter 2 contains several such examples including the shades, blinds, draperies, and cubes, which can either separate or connect each child's territory (see Control of Space/Territoriality).

A Mix of Separation and Connection

We have been arguing that people are influenced by the opposite tendencies of being with others and away from others. It is possible to use design to simultaneously satisfy both motives by creating a mix of separation and connection.

Relationships between people in a designed setting can exist along five different dimensions: visual, acoustic, tactile, olfactory, and symbolic (Zeisel, 1981). Thus, we can either be connected or separated by seeing, hearing, touching, smelling, and/or perceiving.

Perhaps the following account will help make this point more clearly:

I like to go upstairs in my den to write letters and work on the family finances. But, recently, I've been keeping my door open so I can hear the kids and so they know they can bother me if something important comes up.

What seems to work best for this person is a combination of inaccessibility (to take care of business) and accessibility (to monitor the children). The following techniques, which are described more fully in earlier sections of this chapter, can assist us in obtaining such a mixture of separateness and togetherness:

1. Selective control of information about the self/visual distractions and noise: People can be separated by barriers visually, tactually, and symbolically, but may still be able to talk to each other. Masking devices can separate people acoustically, but these people may still be able to see and touch each other.

2. Environmental messages/signs, signals, and symbols: Symbolic territories, defined by color and pattern, give people the feeling that they are in distinct places but allow them to see each other, talk to each other, etc.

3. Psychological escape/psychological separation: Windows, surrogate views, etc. produce psychological or symbolic distance between people sharing common space but still permit sensory connections.

IDENTITY

— 4 —

All of us have a strong need to know ourselves and feel good about who we are. The environment in general, and the home in particular, plays an important role in this process of self-discovery and self-evaluation. In this chapter, we will discuss three different aspects of the relationship between the home and self-identity: the formation of a strong attachment to the home, the home as an external expression of the self, and the contribution of the home to self-esteem.

Attachment

People have a tendency to identify with their surroundings. In this process of identification, attachments are formed to places. These places come to have very special meanings to people and comprise an important part of the complex structure of self-identity.

Certainly the home environment is an integral part of the self. Furthermore, the process of forming a lasting and meaningful attachment to the home can be facilitated through design in the following ways.

Distinctiveness

It is difficult to identify with something if one doesn't see it as being different from other things. Therefore, the goal of each of the design ideas presented in this section is to make the home unique, in some positive way, to facilitate attachment.

Distinctive architectural elements

The following interview is an excellent example of how a unique structural element, a winding staircase, can become part of one's self-image, resulting in a long-lasting attachment to home:

> That house had a winding stairway with a marvelous, ornate bannister. As a child I would slide down it and have visions of someday descending that staircase in a long, lovely dress. It's been years since my parents sold that house, but it holds many wonderful memories.

The client's interview responses concerning previous homes typically are good sources of design features that are already imbued with meaning. These distinctive features from the past can be incorporated into the client's present home, if feasible, or novel elements may be introduced to which future attachments are formed.

Vivid sensory experiences

Designers are certainly quite adept at creating distinctive visual experiences. This practice is quite appropriate as we are primarily "visual animals." Perhaps because of the emphasis upon vision, the other senses can be used quite effectively to provide memorable experiences and meaningful place-attachments.

For example, rooms can be associated with characteristic sounds. Objects such as grandfather clocks and music boxes seem to have much emotional significance. However, interviews revealed that natural sounds are often preferred:

> I fell asleep to the sound of crickets.

> I listened to the pigeons cooing in their roosts on the roof.

> I would like to hear the sound of running water in a garden adjoining my room.

Hall (1966) argues that our memory for places associated with particular smells is much deeper than for those associated with sights or sounds. And, in fact, we have found that people speak longingly of places associated with various odors and fragrances:

I grew up in my grandmother's house which always smelled of a variety of polishes.

I remember the mingling odors of the remains of the evening meal, my grandfather's cigar and perking coffee.

I recall the smell of making wine.

We can also appeal to the most intimate of senses, the sense of touch. Objects and surfaces that people enjoy touching can have special significance to people: "I had a shade which rested on a glass bumpy base which I loved to touch." According to Hall (1966) the memory of tactile experiences also enables us to appreciate texture differences visually: "Contrasts of texture in natural wood, stone, etc. would please my senses."

Different design themes for different rooms

Each member of the household may be asked to choose a design theme for a particular room or area in the home. Then it becomes easier for people to have distinctive emotional experiences in these individualized spaces. And, with proper handling, there can still be a cohesive flow of decorative or design elements which would hold the home together aesthetically (for example, one person's favorite color could dominate in one room and be an accent in another; repeated or coordinated patterns could tie together rooms in which different furniture styles are used).

Dwelling identity

The individuality of the entire home can be emphasized with furnishings that reinforce the historical significance of the house, its architectural style, or the area in which it is located. Some people may even wish to carry this process of authenticating the home to an extreme (for example, by using furniture styles, accessories, art objects, etc. associated with a particular civilization or historical period). Then, the distinctiveness of the home extends to every detail, so that upon entering it, the person is taken back to an earlier time that may have some special meaning.

Participation

Attachments are formed to places that actively involve us. Therefore, each of the following design ideas allows the individual to participate actively with the environment rather than to accept the usual passive role.

Hands-on experiences

Recently, science centers have been designed so that people can experience the effects of touching and manipulating objects and exhibits rather than just passively watching displays and demonstrations. As a result, these places have become extremely popular with both children and adults by creating an active involvement with the environment. Of course, these new museums are particularly attractive because people are usually not allowed to touch things in public places, in contrast to the home environment where active responding is expected.

Still, it may be possible to increase the amount of participation, or encourage involvement in unique ways, in the home as well. For example, there are products on the market that are activated by sound waves (for example, a clock that displays the time when hands are clapped). Other products are activated by touch (for example, a combination table or floor luminaire and planter). You touch the leaves of the plant, and the light turns on.

Examples like the preceding ones may simulate the science-museum experience of discovering novel and surprising ways to affect our surroundings. Then not only can we respond to our environment, but the environment can respond to us. In this way, a strong and harmonious relationship with the home is formed. This process is similar to the way we form attachments to other people, as we see ourselves as both cause and effect of the other's behavior.

Further applications of the concept of control

You may have noticed the similarity between our previous discussion of hands-on experiences and the need for control, as both involve the ability to manipulate the environment. And, in fact, a number of the suggestions that we gave in Chapter 2 not only engender a sense of personal control, but also facilitate attachment to the home through participation. Underdesigned space invites us to participate. Soft architecture encourages us to manipulate. The activity areas for children and adults involve us.

Participation in the design process

It is a lot easier to identify with, and become attached to, places that we have helped to design. Therefore, we strongly suggest that clients be involved in the design process.

Most people are quite eager to participate; however, some may give the appearance, at least initially, of not wanting to be involved. They may say things like: "Hurry up, let's get it over with; whatever you say is fine." These individuals have their own tasks to perform, may have little time to devote to the complexities of design, and are glad to have someone else take over the responsibility for decision making. Ultimately, even these people find it difficult to completely avoid participation, particularly when the topic of color is introduced.

Although the following color preference examples come from our work in office settings, they apply equally well to the residential environment. One client, after remaining on the periphery of earlier discussions, questioned whether a blue leather chair for his desk was appropriate because he wore so many blue suits. Another client, when initially interviewed, made one minor suggestion and said, "Everything else is fine." Later, however, he requested that the color of his sports car be used in his office and even brought in a color sample of the paint. In both cases, the wishes of the client were satisfied without disrupting the overall color scheme.

But, we have heard some designers say: "What do you do if what the client wants is all wrong." That's the beauty of our need-satisfaction approach to design. The client is naturally involved in the design process through the interview. We let people talk about important experiences that they have had, or desire to have, in the home environment. Their needs are explained in the language of the lay person. Clients cannot want things that are wrong because we help them to realize what they really want, and need, in a psychological sense. Our focus on underlying needs, rather than on more superficial and specific design preferences, allows us to avoid the problem. Then, after clients understand what they need psychologically, they are supplied with alternate designs that would work well for them. Thus, we work with people rather than against them, in a process that makes sense to both client and designer.

Personalized design

Furnishings that look and feel as if they have been made by a person are easier to identify with than those that have an assembly-line look. Handmade, hand-carved furniture and accessories would fall in this category. The workmanship and attention to detail make it obvious to the consumer that a craftsman cared enough to spend the time, and make the effort to create something real. Unfortunately, hand-carved furnishings hardly exist in our industrialized technology-oriented society, except for some antiques of formidable expense. Alternatively, we can emphasize a second dimension of personalized design (for instance, personalization through imperfection). People aren't perfect. Sometimes it is their errors that endear them to us. In the same way, we tend to have a feeling of closeness for things that have rough edges or minor irregularities, or are incomplete in some way. For this reason, people may prefer a piece of furniture made by a friend or relative as long as it is competently done. It may not be as symmetrical as a similar piece purchased in a store—it shows some error but, in the process, reveals its humanness. Unfinished furniture may have the same attraction for people.

Similarly, clients themselves can be encouraged to participate in the process of making things for their own environment, at least on a small scale. People are usually reluctant to do so because of self-consciousness and fear of criticism from others, but we may be able to overcome their objections by pointing out the benefits to the individual of having personally made, albeit slightly imperfect, items in the home.

Territoriality

Almost by definition, people become attached to things that belong to them. Therefore, space permitting, we should be strongly recommending to our clients that each member of the household be given clear ownership over separate rooms or areas. Again, the territorial boundary suggestions discussed in Chapter 2 would help to divide shared spaces into uniquely defined spheres of influence.

Self-Definition

People use the environment as a mode of self-expression, communicating to both themselves and to others who they are and who they would like to be. Claire Cooper (1970) argued that the home environment plays a very critical role in this process of self-definition. In fact, the title of her paper, "The House as Symbol of the Self," communicates this message quite well.

More specifically, Cooper maintains that the interior of the home represents the private interior of the person—what a person really is as opposed to one's facade or public image.

Cooper also seems to suggest that the difficulty people have in making design decisions is caused by uncertainty about self-definition, a conclusion that designers have often reached as a function of working with (primarily female) clients in the residential sector. Therefore, we think that interior designers can play an important role in lives of their clients, helping them to clarify the self and objectify it through design. The concepts and procedures presented below may be helpful in performing this task.

However, we certainly are not suggesting that the designer should play the role of the clinical psychologist. As we argued in the chapter on privacy, it's important for people to regulate information about the self, revealing some things and withholding others. Therefore, designers should deal only with aspects of the self (for example, recollections, interests, activities, and aspirations) that are clearly, and voluntarily, revealed by the client interview. Then, treating the person with both respect and sensitivity, we can illustrate the beauty that can be created by designing the home as an expression of the client's individuality. The client can also be given the ability to regulate personal information by participating in decisions concerning which rooms (for instance, public and private) are to be done in this manner.

Personalization

As Cooper (1970) has said: "The furniture we install, the way we arrange it, the pictures we hang, the plants we buy and tend, all are expressions of our image of ourselves . . ." (p. 436). Thus, by personalizing space, the home becomes an external picture of the self—something tangible that we can look at and touch in order to define who we are.

Spaces and surfaces

In order to have the right to display their things, household members must have areas that they own and control. If not, conflicts will inevitably arise as to who can put what, where. In discussing characteristics of ideal future homes, many members of our sample expressed this desire for all people to have a place to express their individuality.

Men have traditionally been given a variety of spaces in the home to personalize (for example, dens, offices, and garages). Women are less likely to have a place of their own. Instead, they have been given the right to decorate the home in general.

This arrangement, however, may be a source of conflict, as the right of children to personalize their own rooms may be usurped by their mothers. Such a theme is expressed by many members of our sample as they recall their childhood home environments. It may be that mothers are expressing their own identities vicariously by decorating their children's rooms. Unfortunately, this behavior conflicts with the need for children to have highly personalized bedrooms as they approach their teen years, a time at which they are struggling to establish a unique identity apart from their parents (Altman and Chemers, 1980; Cooper, 1970).

Perhaps if women are given separate, individualized spaces in the home, they may be more willing to allow their children to personalize their own bedrooms. Then both child and parent benefit, as illustrated by the following personal example:

> My daughter was given essentially empty walls and a plain bedspread. The furnishings, Early American and simple, were okayed by her. She had no sense of style at age six, but I wonder if the fact that I involved her in the choice is the reason she loves authentic old things today? She chose the color of the carpet because it matched her eyes. As she grew, despite the general chaos in the room, her changing interests were displayed on the walls in an orderly fashion. She was fond of saying that she had the best room of any of her friends, and that it was "neat." I learned a lot from observing her; and I really believe that giving her this territory has helped to make her the independent person she is, with a

*strong identity. Although she has warm feelings about her home,
she is quite at home everywhere. By keeping a hands-off policy,
I can now walk into the room where my daughter has grown up
and review her whole childhood on the walls and in the objects.*

Furthermore, in order to facilitate personalization efforts, adequate surfaces must be available in both the horizontal dimension (for example, shelves) and the vertical dimension (for example, bulletin boards). The importance to the individual of prized collections can be highlighted (for example, accented with lighting and framing techniques or showcased in attractive cases and containers). Finally, we recommend surfaces that the client can design, paint, attach things to, etc. in order to increase the input of the person in the process of personalization.

Categories

Before, we mentioned that the designer can help clients to define themselves through design. In order to facilitate this process, the basic client interview can be supplemented with items like the following:

> Write a paragraph describing your image of yourself, your goals, aspirations and interests. Picture yourself in a place that represents who you are and who you would like to be, and describe what that place looks like.

Responses to such items may give us some insight into the client's self-identity and may provide us with clues as to how personalization can be effectively used. However, in order to interpret the data properly, it is helpful to have some system that categorizes the different ways in which people use the environment for self-expression. The personalization categories of Becker and Coniglio (1975), Hansen and Altman (1976), or Zeisel (1981) may be used for this purpose. Alternatively, we have found the following system, based upon the previous ones, quite useful in helping clients make design decisions about their residential interiors.

Association with the past. The past is important to us because it gives definition to the self and meaning to our lives. Therefore, we have found that this category provides a rich source of personalization ideas.

Further insight into our fascination with the past, as well as the measurement of its various dimensions, can be obtained by reading Taylor and Konrad (1980).

In one sense, an association with the past can be reinforced by furnishing a space so that it reflects the client's personal history. Important events, people, and places from the past can be represented in this manner. Generally speaking, we should try to incorporate preferred aspects of previous home environments, revealed in the client interview, into current design in creative and aesthetically pleasing ways.

This tendency to personalize the home in order to reflect earlier satisfying times and experiences is present in a number of our interviews:

> *Today my room still looks like the college dorm rooms I lived in while away at school. There are rock and roll posters still up, along with dilapidated book shelves and orange crates holding my records. All of these are a throwback to my college days. I admit that I still miss that life.*

> *My home is made up of the things I bought during the many trips I've taken. I've enjoyed buying these things and making them part of my home, that which reflects my personality. I'm surrounded by possessions I've enjoyed amassing.*

If the client's ties to the past are particularly strong, an entire room, modeled after a historical museum, may be devoted to an individual and/or family history. This room might be furnished with heirlooms and collected items, which are supplemented with purchases resembling other things that are unavailable. Furnishings, as well as photographs, mementos, etc., can be arranged so that a walk through the room would tell one's personal history in chronological fashion. Areas representing important periods in one's life can be sectioned off to facilitate comparison, so that new insights into one's identity can be formed.

Sometimes, client interviews reveal a different orientation to one's personal past. Adults may try to establish a unique identity by designing their own homes in opposition to their parents' residences. Tognoli and Horwitz (1982), using a residential autobiographic interview similar to ours, have called this process "contradiction." For example, if the childhood home contained small rooms, a desire for a spacious adult home may be expressed. Or if space was traditionally and rigidly defined by parents, the child may develop a preference for greater flexibility and freedom of choice in future residences. Sharing space with siblings may create a strong need for territoriality. Experiencing interruptions and intrusions may result in the desire for more privacy. And being left out of design decisions, as children typically are, may bring out a strong need for control in the adult home.

Designers should examine the relationship between interview descriptions of childhood, current, and future homes very carefully in order to determine whether this contradictory relationship is present. Then, appropriate design decisions can be made that reflect the current identity of the client in relation to the residential history.

In addition to exploring personal history, designers may also wish to collect information on their clients' heritage. Then, furnishings, layouts, colors, fabrics, etc. can be selected to represent national, regional, cultural, ethnic, and/or religious affiliations. Personal interview data can be supplemented by reading Altman and Chemers (1980) and Hall (1966), who offer some excellent examples of, and insights into, the design preferences of various cultural groups.

We have also worked with clients who have formed a very strong attachment to the past by identifying with a particular period in history. Some of these people are willing, and able, to spend quite a bit of money on antiques and on authenticating the home with great attention to detail (for example, duplicating the kinds of nails used in eighteenth-century floor planks).

We certainly can assist in this process of creating a home environment that is both comfortable and comforting for such people, and is central to the self-identity. Additionally, eighteenth-century furnishings can be integrated with modern conveniences to produce a creative synthesis of past and present (for example, period pieces in contemporary fabrics, electrical conveniences with candlelight for atmosphere, and wood-plank floors with a protective coating).

The present: interests, activities, and values.   It is quite common for people to collect and display objects, symbols, and posters and to select furniture styles, colors, and patterns that reflect current definitions of self.

For example, both children and adults personalize space in order to express their current activities and interests:

> *Every year I purchase an attractive calendar so that I can keep a record of the important happenings of my life.*

> *I used my bookcases to display my dolls and other little collections.*

A person's interests can even function as a personalization theme for an entire room:

Above my bureau sit three yellow shelves suspended from the wall, which contain my proudest possessions. Drawings of ships, sea scenes, and Bay workboats dominate. On these shelves also sits my collection of wooden nautical figurines, shells, corals, driftwood, and starfish. The nautical theme is expressed throughout my entire room. Three walls are a brilliant green and one a dazzling yellow. On one wall hangs a large painting of a seaman.

Of course, designers can assist clients in the personalization process by selecting appropriate furnishings, colors, etc., and by suggesting attractive displays and arrangements of space. For instance, green may not have been the best color choice for "the room with a nautical theme" because of its association with land and foliage. Instead, a designer might have recommended the use of blues, slate blues, blue-greens, and sand tones.

Design elements that represent important parts of the self should also have value commensurate with their centrality to the person. Thus, the following individual needed the proper stereo equipment to express her strong interest in music in the fullest sense:

Music was becoming a big part of my life. Unfortunately, I only had a dinky little record player [then]. Music is still one of the biggest things in my life, so I now own a beautiful stereo system.

In a similar vein, personalization of space may be used to represent important milestones in one's life. A child may be presented with a desk to symbolize the passage from the casual play of kindergarten to the more serious learning experiences of the first grade. An adult member of our sample described how he personalized an area of his home to represent an important achievement (for instance, obtaining the Ph.D.):

After I received my doctorate, I furnished a part of my basement with an expensive desk, a swivel chair and library shelves. My diplomas are in frames on the wall above my desk.

Areas of the home can also be personalized to reflect what people believe in—what they value in a social, political, economic, or philosophical sense. Sayings, thoughts, proverbs, etc. can be displayed attractively on walls and other surfaces. For example, one subject described a mantle carved in attractive lettering which said Tis Home Where The Hearth Is. Ecology signs and posters can be displayed to express a pro-environmental attitude. Even the amount of embellishment in the home can be influenced by one's value system. Thus, Weisner and Weibel (1981) concluded that people who have antitechnological attitudes, and value "a lifestyle of contemplation and meditation," may prefer a home that is furnished simply and contains few decorative items.

The future: goals, aspirations, and dreams. In addition to reflecting past associations and current concerns, personalization efforts can have a future orientation. Moos (1976) suggests that people select environments to facilitate personal growth in particular directions. Thus, areas of the home can be designed in order to represent the type of person one wishes to become.

Parents may be able to make a positive contribution to their child's personal development by visually reinforcing expressed goals. The following example illustrates this point:

> *I placed a piano, which my daughter had expressed an interest in learning how to play, directly in her line of vision from her bed. When she awoke, sat up and looked out of her room, she saw the piano. She used to get out of bed literally and go to it and play.*

Furniture, color, fabrics, objects, pictures, and posters can all be combined in a child's room to define goals, provide inspiration, and give pleasure:

> *I remember having a dream of someday being a ballerina. I had a small bedroom that my mom fixed up, and even now it still makes me smile when I think about it. I had a canopy bed with a sheer white top and bed covers. All my furniture was white with gold trim. I had a vanity table with the same white sheer beautiful skirt and matching curtains. I had ballerina pictures and objects all around. It was great. It was my dream.*

With respect to adults, a work space for the achievement of certain goals can be incorporated into the design concept for any room. Initial design guidelines can be obtained from interview data, specifically from what clients say about their desires for an ideal future home. For example, a client may say something like: "I would like a larger and more comfortable work area so as to be more productive in the future."

Opportunities for Privacy

In the previous chapter, we argued that there are times at which it is appropriate for people to separate themselves from others. When we are alone, we can experience ourselves as autonomous human beings. We can attend closely to what we are thinking and feeling. We can reflect upon the events of the day, work out problems, and plan for the future. Thus, a solitude experience can be an occasion for obtaining self-knowledge and enhancing self-identity.

The section of Chapter 3 on social withdrawal is a good source of design concepts for producing physical and/or psychological separation for this purpose. However, we would like to add one additional idea, which seems particularly appropriate for the process of self-reflection. A separate room, which is too small to be used for regular activities, or even a large, properly ventilated closet, can become a private room for meditation and reflective problem solving.

Whenever a problem arises, we would "visit" our problem-solving room. In this manner, problems, worries, etc. could be "confined" to this small space, reserving other areas of the home for more productive, pleasant, and relaxing activities. How many sleepless nights this procedure would prevent! If a problem is keeping us awake, we would just get up, go to our private space, think over the problem, solve it, or reserve solution for some later visit; and then, when ready, go back to bed. Then, the bedroom would be associated with feelings of relaxation, thus facilitating sleep.

Self-Evaluation

Besides knowing who we are (self-definition), it is important to feel good about ourselves (self-evaluation). People would like to think of themselves as worthwhile, competent human beings. Therefore, the goal of the design concepts presented in this section is to help people achieve a positive image of self.

Design Quality

Much has been written about the relationship between housing quality and the self-concept. Ladd (1976), in summarizing this literature, states that the house is a tangible symbol of a person's self-worth. Although most of this work is concerned with the exterior, structural aspects of housing, as well as the quality of the surrounding neighborhood, the designer can maximize the quality of the interior environment and, thus, also help to raise the self-esteem of its occupants. In fact, people may be in a better position to alter the interior design of their homes, whereas they may be somewhat constrained in moving from a particular house or neighborhood. One member of our sample discussed such a situation. The neighborhood, which had once been a well-respected community, had deteriorated over the years. A number of factors prevented relocation; however, this person was able to maintain a feeling of pride by making the interior of the home beautiful.

In order to help people achieve positive feelings of self, we can determine the client's own definition of quality by means of the interview and make recommendations as to what is generally valued. With a small budget we might suggest the purchase of one special object, perhaps a painting or a rich fabric for pillows or upholstery. Or, finances permitting, a room may be filled with aesthetic objects and furnishings that use the best materials, represent workmanship, or have labels on them—like clothing—to advertise their designers.

In another sense, design quality may be closely related to cleanliness, particularly for women. For example, a member of our sample was asked, "If your kitchen could talk, what would it say?" The response was: "I feel good about how ——— takes care of me; I sparkle." In other words, there is an implication that taking good care of the kitchen results in feelings of self-worth. The residential interviews of Becker and Coniglio (1975) also revealed that "the cleanliness of the home is a reflection of the family and, more particularly, the wife" (p. 62).

Thus, it follows that anything that is done to facilitate the care and maintenance of the home will help its residents feel good about themselves (for example, easy-to-clean surfaces and appliances and time-saving, automated housekeeping devices). More extensive and detailed suggestions are presented in Chapter 6: Household Maintenance

Territoriality

Earlier in this chapter, we noted that control over space facilitates environmental attachments and contributes to self-definition through personalization. It is also true that the act of giving a member of the household a personal territory is a way of granting status to the individual and of signaling the acceptance of the person by others. Similarly, Altman (1975) hypothesizes that "the absence of a primary territory . . . may well yield, in the long run, a lack of self-esteem" (p. 112). These arguments serve to strengthen our strong recommendation that all family members be given some place in the home to own, control, and personalize.

Privacy

We also mentioned earlier in this chapter that solitary experiences contribute to self-definition, as we can get to know ourselves better when we are alone. Additionally, we evaluate ourselves during these private moments, a process that may lead to greater self-acceptance.

One subject described the den as "a little retreat," a room in which the person escapes into another world, reads for pleasure, works on personal business, and has private discussions with visiting children. This person also told us that if the room could talk, it would say: "I like myself." This response suggests that a room reserved for privacy not only is an enjoyable, favorite place to be, but also is a place that we can go in order to feel good about ourselves. Design concepts for this purpose are discussed in the social withdrawal section of the privacy chapter.

Furthermore, an effective person can successfully control information about the self, prevent interference with one's activities, and regulate the amount of achieved privacy appropriately. Therefore, additional ideas for designing a place that makes one feel good as a person can be found in the corresponding sections of Chapter 3.

Environmental Control

There is a very close relationship between the ability to manipulate the environment and feelings of personal competence. Alternatively, unpredictable and uncontrollable environments represent threats to human dignity. Therefore, the design concepts developed in Chapter 2 in order to increase environmental control are also relevant here, when it comes to enhancing the individual's conception of self.

At a minimum, we can recommend to clients the use of furnishings and ambient environmental control devices that can be easily manipulated to fit various tasks and activities. Having an opportunity to pursue hobbies and interests in the home can certainly help a person feel worthwhile.

Furthermore, we can create designs and recommend the purchase of objects and devices that fit a person's physical and mental capacities.

Perhaps nothing is as frustrating, or as demeaning to our humanness, as a machine that defeats us because we can't make it work as intended. The following account is instructive in this regard:

> *The remote control for our TV went out of whack, and the sound got louder and louder. Although there is a manual control back-up, it didn't work. I couldn't turn it off, and the increasing din of voices made me react in a frantic way. I needed the remote to control the set, but it wouldn't. I wound up throwing the darn thing into the next room and pulling the plug on the TV. It was like a robot gotten out of hand. It took me over. And its small size was partly responsible for my feeling of helplessness. We have not replaced it because I will not use one again. I not only felt incompetent but a little crazed.*

As you can see, it makes sense for machines and appliances to have properly designed manual controls. Our next "story" indicates that controls should also be properly labeled so people can understand their functions.

> *I was alone in my friend's home, and I wanted to turn on some music. They had complex stereo tape-cassette/record playing-FM radio equipment. No instructions were available to me, so I had to depend on the names under each of the knobs. The time required to read these designations on the control panel was ten minutes, including the time it took to find a magnifying lens to read the small lettering while crouching on the floor. Some knobs made sense, such as bass, treble, volume and balance. Some made "half" sense. Do you use the "selector" knob to change the station? To me, AFC means automatic frequency control but to another, unfamiliar with the letter designation,*

perhaps nothing. I suppose "record" and "play" were for the cassette. But, I could not, out of the eight or ten knobs, figure out how to turn it on. There was no on/off knob. Finally, I decided to try the knob which said "power." It worked. I was afraid to damage the equipment. I was unfamiliar with the complexity. And, I was so frustrated that I didn't initially associate power with on/ off.

The preceding examples illustrate problems that all of us may have, at one time or another, in dealing with an inhuman technology that demeans us by failing to take our human characteristics and limitations into account. Special populations (for example, the aged, infirm, and handicapped) are particularly at risk in this regard. We must be sensitive to their special needs and corresponding design requirements.

Raschko's (1982) book on housing interiors is very helpful in designing a supportive, therapeutic home environment that fosters positive feelings of self-sufficiency and independence for elderly and disabled individuals. This excellent text provides guidelines for such things as the selection and arrangement of furnishings, the use of prosthetic devices, and the design of mechanical systems in the living room, the kitchen, the bathroom, and the bedroom. A variety of useful suggestions are presented with the goal of maximizing comfort (for example, sedentary individuals need chairs that remain comfortable over extended periods of time), aesthetics (for example, institutional-appearing furnishings should be avoided), safety (for example, flammable upholstery fillers are not appropriate for people who are slow to respond to emergencies), accessibility (for example, devices such as adjustable counter tops and front-loading dishwashers with pull-out racks increase one's reach zone), and controllability (for example, water flow in the bath can be controlled by a single lever that operates a water mixer).

Design decisions must also take into account the special needs of children so that they may move about the home in an independent way. Accessibility is certainly important in this regard. Storage spaces should be within reach; or devices, such as ladders, should be provided to increase the child's ability to get at things easily without having to ask for help. With respect to clothing storage, children can have custom-designed closets, with racks and shelves adjustable as to height, so that the closet grows with them. Light switches could even be lowered.

Children can also be given accessibility to objects by providing them with possessions that are similar to the ones their parents have (for example, inexpensive, but real, substitutes such as radios, clocks, cameras, pens, etc.). Giving the young control over such objects allows them to function in an autonomous manner; they don't have to be continually asking for permission to use things.

In a similar manner, children should be given the freedom to manipulate the environment without having to worry about breaking things or damaging them. Then, rather than being demeaned by restrictions on the use of objects and failures to use them properly, they can experience positive feelings of self as environmental competencies develop.

For example, washable surfaces on walls and furnishings can be used in the child's room. Laminated surfaces and lacquer finishes can be damaged whereas wood, on the other hand, can be refinished. And, if children are given nice things, they will generally learn to take care of them because they were considered worthy and responsible enough to do so by their parents.

Of course, it is necessary to keep some things in the home that are breakable or dangerous, in such rooms as the kitchen or bath. These things can be stored well out of the reach of children in a decorative cabinet or can be protected by the use of decorative locks.

SECURITY

— 5 —

It is necessary for our well-being to have a place in which our psychological and physical security is assured. Certainly, at a minimum, the home should fulfill this need. Therefore, in this chapter, we will demonstrate how design can contribute to feelings of security by creating a home environment that nurtures and protects its residents, is characterized by permanence and stability, and is free of accidents and other hazards.

Nurturance

When people are at home, they like to feel that it is a warm, cozy, and comfortable place to be. In fact, many members of our sample use such adjectives to describe the ideal home environment as a place in which they feel taken care of, nurtured, and protected. The concepts to follow should be helpful in designing residential interiors so that this "maternal" role is fulfilled.

Family/Child-Oriented Environments

The home may have acquired the capacity for nurturance because it is a setting in which nurturant activities occur. In other words, the feelings of warmth and safety that we had as children, being taken care of by our parents, are transferred to the home. In a similar vein, Cooper (1970) sees the home as an extension of the womb. Initially, the mother is the "whole environment" of the infant; but as the child develops, the surrounding physical environment (for instance, the home) takes on this role as "a place of security and love." Weisner and Weibel (1981), in their survey of family life styles, found that some homes had a very strong child orientation. These homes were decorated in such a manner that the nurturant function is accented. Such an approach may be appropriate for clients with young children for two reasons: A nurturant home recognizes the importance of children and, thus, contributes to their feelings of security, and this family emphasis also results in a secure environment for adults. Parents can not only care for their children comfortably in such a place but can also re-experience the feelings of warmth and security associated with their own childhood as they engage in nurturant behavior themselves.

Children's rooms

We can accomplish these goals by designing special rooms for children (for example, nurseries, play areas, etc.). Because the presence of such rooms may be sufficient to satisfy the need for security, they can be designed to meet other needs that are revealed in the client interview. For example, Weisner and Weibel (1981) described a home with "a newly and brightly painted nursery overflowing with toys, books, and puzzles, homely, comfortable chairs, homemade quilts, and afghans on rocker seats" (p. 435). This high complexity interior may work well for a child with a strong need for environmental stimulation (see Chapter 7). Alternatively, the room may be filled with soft architectural furnishings, to satisfy the need for control, or visually protected spaces, to satisfy the need for privacy. It may be a place of play and fantasy for emotional release or a highly personalized bedroom that expresses the unique identity of a child. Generally speaking, any of the children's rooms we have described in other chapters could be used to increase the family centeredness of the home.

Integrating children and adults

An environment that accepts and welcomes the child also has places for children in family areas. Such an arrangement may result in feelings of warmth and security that can be shared by all family members. These feelings are expressed so beautifully by the following recollection:

I remember sitting in an overstuffed armchair in the corner of my grandparents' and parents' kitchen/dining area, feeling very safe, warm and loved, and listening to them discussing the day's events. Many evenings I remember falling asleep in that chair, all curled up, and my father carrying me into my bed.

The child's territory could be located in any room where the family regularly gathers. The boundaries of the child's space can be defined by objects: pillows that the child can arrange or even a full-size "grownup" chair with down-filled cushions so that the child can feel a part of the adult world.

Besides fulfilling the nurturance component of security, this arrangement may also teach children respect for the territory and property of other family members.

Children can also be welcomed into other parts of the home. A special chair, built for two, in the parents' bedroom would be nice for curling up with mommy or daddy. A boudoir chair, selected by the parents for their own use, could also serve this purpose. If there isn't enough room for a chair perhaps the bed will do. Children generally love to tumble about or be cuddled there: "My mother used to toss me in the sheets when the bedding was changed."

The design challenge here is to select bedding that is not only comfortable and inviting but can also withstand wear and tear. Then, adults will feel no anxiety about fabrics being mussed or worn, and children will feel free to use the furnishing in any way that feels good. Quilts are good choices for bed coverings as they are soft, warm, pliable, and washable.

Older children may even be given a special furnishing to use when visiting the den or home office of one of the parents. Of course, the parent would determine when such a visit is appropriate so that privacy would not be violated. In fact, the periodic visits themselves would reinforce a healthy respect for adult privacy and work. And how privileged the child would feel to be so honored.

Displays

Children's art and other objects may also be prominently displayed in social areas of the home. Of course, it is necessary to be somewhat selective in this regard so that the overall aesthetics of the space are not disturbed. By providing appropriate explanations as to what can and cannot be included, and how these things can be arranged, we may help children develop a sense of order and some aesthetic understanding.

It is quite common for parents to decorate their refrigerators with the drawings of their children. Carrying the idea further, a screen can be covered with a collage of drawings and paintings, or a display case can be designed so that arts and crafts work can be changed easily to reflect the development of the child's skills over time.

Displays can also communicate family cohesiveness and continuity. The following design elements observed by Weisner and Weibel (1981) in child-oriented homes seem to serve this function: family portraits, a painting commemorating the birth of a child, a mother's infant dishes and books.

Additionally, the interests of all family members can be displayed together in a single, accessible, public region. A collection of sports objects (for example, father's jogging shoes, mother's tennis racket, daughter's ice skates, and son's football) can be placed near a door, family room, or garage in a neat and attractive manner rather than being stashed away in each person's closet. This arrangement of space represents each person's uniqueness but also tells á more important story: Although we might not share all activities, we are still a secure family unit. We care about each other. Each of us feels wanted, needed, appreciated, and accepted.

Intimate family spaces

Finally, we would like to point out that there is a close relationship between sociability, nurturance, and security. Note the following interview:

> For my family the kitchen has always been a combination living room-den-kitchen. . . . We always seem to congregate [there]. . . . It has always been a warm, cozy room. . . . The room gives me a sense of warmth and security.

Accordingly, we think that a nurturant home should include areas specifically designed for experiencing family intimacy. Many of our subjects, including the previous one, see the kitchen as such a place. In fact, the kitchen seems to be a natural setting for satisfying the security need because of its association with the fulfillment of the basic need for nourishment in both a biological and psychological sense. The preparation of food and the sharing of the meal allow all family members to participate in a nurturant environment. But the kitchen must serve a variety of functions:

*My kitchen/dining area now is ultramodern and streamlined. I
love it for its conveniences, clean look, and workability. What I
do miss is the warm feeling of the past and consider my present
kitchen only as a working area.*

What can we learn from the previous example? Well, for one thing, a
modern, functional, efficient kitchen may lack the ability to provide a
warm, nurturing family atmosphere. But, it is also apparent from this interview that we need to consider order and organization (see Chapter 6), as
well as sociability (Chapter 10) and security in the design of a kitchen.

How can we do all that in a single space? Our subject offered one potential solution to the problem by suggesting that the kitchen be differentiated into several areas: "My ideal kitchen/dining area would be modern
and built for convenience, but would have an area in it that would provide
an intimate conversation corner."

Multifunctional design elements, such as the cutting-board island in
the following example, can also be used to simultaneously satisfy several
needs:

*My kitchen has a working area and an eating area separated by a
cutting-board island, which serves as the main working area. . . .
Our family sits around the table a lot. My husband works there.
Sometimes when my children were home, they also used the
kitchen to work in. . . . When we are all together, we can eat in
the kitchen and use the cutting board island as a server.*

The cutting board in the preceding example is functional since it acts
as a work surface for preparing and serving food. It also organizes space by
defining separate work and social areas. But the cutting board, as a partial
waist-high barrier, also connects the family members at the table with the
person preparing the meal.

Alternatively, personalization details (for example, colors, fabrics,
towels, pot holders, and pictures) can be added to an otherwise functionally
oriented kitchen to "humanize the mechanics" and, thus, create a feeling of
warmth, security, and friendliness.

Of course, intimate family spaces can be created in other parts of the
home (see Chapter 10 for additional ideas). General guidelines for both the
location and the design of these areas can be obtained from the interview. In
this way, we can be responsive to the client's unique conception of inti-
macy/nurturance.

Feeling of Enclosure

Perhaps you have noticed that infants prefer to curl up in the corner of a crib and, in fact, may be even happier in a laundry basket, cradle, bassinet, or carriage. Are these tight spaces preferred because they resemble the security of the womb? Cooper (1970) seems to suggest such a relationship and points out further that some "organic architects" have tried "to re-create this safe, enclosed, encircling feeling in their designs" (p. 441).

Children also prefer small, bounded spaces. Our interview data indicates such a preference as a number of subjects recalled quite vividly how they constructed various types of enclosures:

When we were children, I would make my bed into a tent by putting sheets or blankets on the bed posts. Then, all of us would get under and pretend that it was our own little house. I remember feeling very warm and protected there.

Teenagers and young adults show the same tendency: "I have my bed up on the dressers, making a space underneath where I have a beanbag chair and small table." In fact, a careful analysis of our data reveals that people, at all stages of the life cycle, consistently associate small, enclosed spaces with feelings of protection and security.

Designers can incorporate such areas into the home environment by taking advantage of natural enclosures such as corners (described by one subject as "little pockets of comfort"), eaves, slanted ceilings, and areas under stairwells. An infant or child would certainly be happy there. But, the space could also be filled with furnishings appropriate to an adult seeking a place of security.

Effective enclosures in other locations can also be created by using the boundary techniques discussed in Chapter 2. Alternatively, furniture can be used for the same purpose (for example, canopy beds and chairs). For example, a chair that envelops the person (for example, Saarinen's "womb chair" and Jacobsen's "egg chair") often becomes a favorite place for sitting, reading, thinking, etc.:

We had a round-backed chair I bought for the basement when we had a TV down there. I had to move it into the living room to make room for other furnishings. My husband took it over. In fact, everyone takes it over—first come, first serve. Your arms can stretch out on the frame. You can turn and twist and curl up if you like. It's a superior, secure chair.

Comfortable Furniture

The feeling of being nurtured in the enclosures that we have recommended can be further enhanced by filling them with soft architectural elements (for example, down-filled pillows, blankets, stuffed animals for children, and smooth velvet or silky satinlike fabrics).

We also recommend upholstered seating with soft covers and pliable fillers for any location because people seem to associate comfortable seating that they can sink into with feelings of protection and safety.

Warmth

Many of our subjects associated being warm in a physical sense with being protected:

> *I remember falling asleep on the living room floor in front of the heat register. It was very warm and made me feel secure.*

> *I like to get into a nice hot tub when it's a cold and blustery day. I feel very warm and cozy.*

> *We had a sun parlor that I liked to be in. It gave me a very secure feeling.*

These interviews suggest that warmth/temperature can be produced naturally, by designing rooms to take advantage of the sun, or artificially with equipment such as electric blankets, hot tubs, saunas, fireplaces, wood-burning stoves, and other climate control devices.

Floors can be covered with thick pile or shag carpets, fur or synthetic fur rugs, etc. to avoid the following experience: "Winters were cold when I got out of bed, and I hated the run to the bathroom across the cold parquet floor."

People are also warmed by the touch of certain fabrics: "Many afternoons I would jump onto my chenille spread and feel its warmth." Therefore, chenille, velvet, fur, and down-filling would be good choices for spreads, quilts, blankets, or throws.

Color

Generally, research into the relationship between color and mood suggests that people associate cool colors with feelings of security. Wexner (1954), for example, found that blue is seen as a "soothing" and "secure" color. Children prefer cooler colors as they develop greater emotional control (Alschuler and Hattwick, 1947). College students also associate blues and greens with "calm, security and peace" (Sharpe, 1975).

However, most of these experiments are based upon the analysis of group averages. Clients whose color associations differ from "the average person" will, most likely, be encountered. One of our subjects, for example, said that blue gave him "a rather cold and sterile feeling." This same person had "a warm, comfortable feeling" in his family room, which was done in "deep, warm colors--tones of orange and brown."

This example illustrates that research results cannot be indiscriminantly applied; individual differences must be taken into account. Colors acquire particular associations on the basis of prior experience and cultural background. Clients can be questioned about these meanings and feelings. Some answers to these questions may be provided by the interview questions that we have already suggested. If not, clients can be asked specifically about their reactions to colors that they have experienced in past and present home environments.

Alternatively, an adjective checklist may be used in which clients are shown color samples and are asked to check off the adjectives that describe their perceptions of the colors. A checklist can be generated for this purpose, which includes adjectives that suggest security (for example, warm, comfortable, soft, secure, safe, protected, and cozy) mixed in with irrelevant filler items (for example, complex, clear, spacious, permanent, specialized, beautiful, and ornate). On the basis of the results, colors that have connotations of security for the individual client can be selected.

Personalization

Becker and Coniglio (1975) found that over 90 percent of their subjects attempted to make a new residence "comfortable" and "homelike" through personalization of some form. This result suggests that the techniques for personalizing the home, presented in Chapter 3, not only contribute to our sense of identity, but also make us feel more secure.

Consequently, designers can act as consultants, assisting their clients in the creation of appropriately personalized spaces. As an example, note how the following subject has decorated her room so that it nurtures and protects her: "I would do my bedroom in a Laura Ashley style; I'd want it cozy, ruffly, pastely, [in pastel colors] so I could curl up in it."

Permanence

Toffler (1970) has written eloquently about a rather frightening condition which taxes our powers of adaptation—future shock. We are exposed to a rapidly changing technological world in which familiar places may be destroyed and relationships are often short-lived. Living under such circumstances, it is not surprising that our lives have a feeling of "temporariness" about them. However, designers can help people combat this feeling of "transience" and "impermanence" by creating a secure atmosphere of roots and stability in the home environment.

Association with the Past

Taylor and Konrad (1980) have noted that the past is becoming increasingly important to us. We work to prevent the destruction of historic buildings and preserve attractive older sections of our cities. We shop at antique stores and flea markets.

But what accounts for our recent fascination with the past? Although there are a number of reasons for this phenomenon, we agree with Taylor and Konrad, who argue that people attempt to preserve the past as a way of coping with future shock. The past provides us with anchors by representing what is familiar and secure in an uncertain world. Therefore, we recommend that designers help people achieve a meaningful connection with the past by using the following techniques.

Personal history

As we have mentioned earlier, many of our subjects attempt to recreate preferred aspects of their childhood home(s) in the present. Now perhaps you can understand why—if you consider our discussion of the future-shock concept. In fact, a number of our subjects clearly articulated the relationship between the preservation of their personal past and the need for security: "I remember my childhood home to be a very safe and pleasant place, one that I have tried to reconstruct for my own family."

If we pay close attention to client descriptions of homes from the past and their relationship to the present and the future, we may be able to incorporate elements from previously secure places into current home environments. Then, color, lighting, furnishings, layouts, etc. can be used to create a sense of continuity with the client's personal history.

People also collect artifacts to preserve important events and places from the past that have undergone transformation (for example, a brick from a high school that has been torn down to make way for a new building or equipment from a defunct railroad that provided many years of satisfying employment). Designers may be able to facilitate this process of preserving precious memories by integrating items that remind their clients of the past into the overall aesthetics of the home. Additional design ideas and examples for using the client's personal past as a personalization category are presented in Chapter 4.

Antiquarianism

People are often comforted by surrounding themselves with objects from their personal past. It is also true that an association with old things in general can add to our feelings of permanence and security. According to McKechnie (1977), this "antiquarian" tendency includes an "enjoyment of antiques and historical places," a "preference for traditional versus modern design," and an "appreciation of cultural artifacts of earlier eras." In a similar manner, Taylor and Konrad (1980) speak of the importance of directly experiencing the past. One of the items that they use to measure this tendency describes the characteristics of an antiquarian home quite well: "I would be happy living in an old house full of antique furniture and mementos of the past."

Our own interview data provide additional insights into the relationship between the past and the need for permanence. One person thought that having a contemporary home "interspersed with antique accessories" would give it "a warmer feeling." Another felt secure in the fact that her furniture was older than she was.

Substance

Big, heavy pieces of furniture and sturdy building materials connote permanence and stability. One subject, for example, took comfort in her "old substantial house with heavy wood frames on doors and windows, and wood floors."

Similarly, Hall (1966) mentions that Germans prefer double doors and heavy chairs to their "flimsy" and "lightweight" counterparts in our culture.

In order to understand these feelings better, let's consider what the following individual had to say about a home from his past:

I remember a big, floor-model radio in my grandparents' home. It was in the corner of the living room against the wall. As a child, I used to sit there on the floor listening to my favorite radio programs. There was something special about that radio. I felt so secure there. I didn't have the same feeling listening to the little radio in the breakfast room. And I have never had that same feeling listening to the portable, transistor radios of the present.

What was so special about that old radio? Its size gave stature and importance to the act of listening, and its lack of portability defined a permanent, secure place in the home. Perhaps people feel that the home and the family will endure if things of substance are included in its design.

The preceding interview also suggests that the concept of substance may be in conflict with the soft architecture approach advocated in Chapter 2. In other words, characteristics of soft architecture such as flexibility and portability allow us to manipulate environments conveniently, but don't have the same connotation of permanence as things that don't change and can't move.

If the client interview reveals that the needs for control and security are both present, designers may not want to use the soft architecture approach for furnishings. But the client's specific associations should be clearly ascertained. Does the client perceive lightweight furniture as "flimsy"? If so, a heavier piece can be used to define "a place" within a room. Then, the security need is satisfied by the concept of substance, and the need for control by defining the boundaries of a territory with an object.

Symbols of Home

> There were benches surrounding the fireplace. The mantle was carved in attractive lettering and said Tis Home Where the Hearth Is. It was a great place to gather together around the fire with family and friends. When we did I felt as though I would live in that house forever.

We think that the preceding subject has said something important about the relationship between home, security, and permanence in the description of the childhood home. The design of this living room area combines a number of elements that make a house homelike by symbolizing its permanence. These symbols of home include an intimate seating area for family and friends, the fireplace, and the display of artwork representing home and hearth.

The use of such symbols may be particularly appropriate for those people who have experienced many moves in the past and, therefore, have developed the need for a stable home base. In these cases, family gathering areas can be designed to symbolize home, using ideas from the previously described living room, other universal symbols (for example, candlelight, flowers on the dining table, and pleasant cooking odors circulating throughout the house), or appropriate simulations (for example, a lighting scheme that simulates firelight, and fragrance discs).

Safety

At a minimum, the home should be a safe place—one that is free of accidents, hazards, and unwanted intrusions. This need is so basic that many people fail to mention it in the context of considering design changes to the home; very few of our subjects talked about safety concerns in their interviews. On the other hand, designers, who are used to meeting safety standards in choosing fabrics, equipment, lighting, and electrical plans, may have to remind their clients of the importance of residential security.

Safety Features

We will not attempt to generate an exhaustive list of safety features for the residential environment in this section. Other references are available for that purpose which we will mention later. Instead, we would like to give some general advice about typical client preferences and reactions, and discuss the proper role for designers in making recommendations with respect to safety issues.

Many clients put aesthetic preferences above practical safety matters, insisting on attractive kitchen floors that, unfortunately, can become slippery if liquid spills on them (for example, ceramic tile and quarry tile). In such cases, designers should point out the potential hazards and suggest alternatives that are both aesthetically pleasing and safe.

This role of raising consciousness with respect to safety hazards is a proper one for designers, particularly when dealing with clients who have young children. Designers can involve their clients in a reassuring discussion of safety issues, pointing out some of the things to avoid in order to cut down on home accidents (for example, sharp corners on tables and other furnishings).

Along the same line, we have found that clients are typically uninformed about fire hazards and fire protection in the home. For example, they may be unaware of the flammability of many materials. Some untreated synthetics, when exposed to flame or excessive heat, burn up quickly, whereas fire-retardant fabrics (for example, wool) smolder and burn slowly, giving people time to react. These needed seconds may be particularly critical to people of limited capacity (for example, small children, the aged, and the handicapped).

In addition to making recommendations about fabrics, we can also discuss how technology can be used to provide additional protection against fires. For example, smoke detectors can be wired to master control units so that lights will come on all over the house, revealing safe routes of escape and warning the hard of hearing of the emergency. Raschko's (1982) book on designs for elderly and disabled individuals has many more specific suggestions concerning home safety that, although generally helpful, are particularly appropriate for these populations.

We have also found that Rooney's (1980) book on home lighting is useful to designers in devising a lighting plan that suits client needs and situational requirements. Material is presented on illuminating both interior (for example, attics and basements) and exterior (for example, steps and walkways) problem areas. Other safety issues, such as wiring, glare, and lights for security, are also treated.

In conclusion, designers should be, and typically are, concerned with residential safety in all their interactions with clients. However, we must be particularly sensitive to the safety needs of those people who have a high need for security. Some clients reveal information that suggests the salience of this need; for example they may mention in the interview such experiences as falling down the stairs, slipping in the tub, etc.

For these people, perhaps even one unfortunate incident can change the meaning of the home from a place of security and relaxation to one of anxiety and stress. Furthermore, some need-hierarchy personality theorists (for example, Maslow, 1954) suggest that higher-level needs, such as belongingness and self-esteem, cannot be addressed as long as lower-level needs, such as safety, go unsatisfied. Therefore, people in general, and high security-need individuals in particular, need our understanding and can benefit from our knowledge with respect to safety considerations in the home environment.

Crime-Proofing

Much time, effort, and money can be spent in trying to "crime-proof" the home with dead-bolt locks, window grates, burglar alarms, and total security systems. Designers can help their clients make choices by providing information about alternative devices, seeing that their installation doesn't add a prisonlike quality to the home and, most importantly, by discussing the consequences of their use.

Some clients may reveal a high fear of crime in their interviews, a concern that is probably related to the perceived safety of the neighborhood. For example, one member of our sample said:

I have lived in my present home for many years. When I moved in, the neighborhood was a pleasant place to live. Now the community is not as safe as it used to be.

Perhaps the use of security devices may help such a person feel more secure in the home. However, Sommer (1974), in discussing public environments, makes some very interesting points about this "security state of mind." For one thing, this approach may not work because some intruders may simply be challenged by the presence of security equipment rather than being deterred by it. This outcome makes sense if, as Rossman and Ulehla (1977) argue, seeking out challenge and risk is one of the motives for engaging in urban crime.

Furthermore, Sommer contends that the presence of security devices sensitizes people to their lack of safety. In other words, people may conclude that: "If it's necessary for me to install locks, alarms, etc., this place must really be unsafe." Paradoxically, we may then feel less safe than we did before.

Considering Sommer's arguments perhaps it would be best not to bring up the security/crime issue unless it is mentioned by the client. We wouldn't want to create unnecessary anxiety. However, if the client volunteers information about recent neighborhood crime problems, a discussion of the pros and cons of security devices in the home would be in order.

ORDER

— 6 —

It is quite common for psychologists in the areas of personality, social, and environmental psychology to describe the personalities of both people and places in terms of the need for order. For example, Jackson's (1967) Personal Research Form is a paper-and-pencil personality test that measures a variety of individual traits including order, defined as a concern "with keeping personal effects and surroundings neat and organized," and a dislike for "clutter, confusion, and lack of organization" (p. 7). S. Kaplan (1975) argues that we must be able to make sense of our environment in order to adapt to it successfully. Accordingly, we prefer places that are high in order, structure, and coherence. Ratings of building aspects are also influenced by an organization factor (Hershberger, 1970).

In this chapter, we will describe a number of design concepts for each of three different aspects of the need for order: perceptual organization, household maintenance, and organization of activities.

Perceptual Organization

Here we are concerned with the way things look to people. Is the home well organized? Can patterns be perceived? Is the environment characterized by balance, symmetry, and clarity? Does the organization of the home make sense? Or are things arranged haphazardly? Are there gaps and inconsistencies? Is the environment confusing and cluttered?

Grouping

According to Gestalt psychologists, we have a natural tendency to categorize elements of the environment. We see some things as being members of a common group and other things as being separate from each other.

This need to impose some sort of order upon the perceptual world is evident in the following subject's interview:

> *I remember my bedroom . . . as having black, red, and white wallpaper with matching curtains set off by red carpeting. It provided a sense of order, which was needed at the time. My bedroom now is very noncontrived but is put together with a total color scheme which balances it out to create continuity. [In the future] I picture myself in a bedroom which . . . would still be tied together by color to again provide some sense of order.*

The preceding subject grouped things together on the basis of color— a common tendency. Below are listed a variety of grouping strategies that people regularly use to make sense of their surroundings.

These variables may be familiar as designers have been using them in connection with aesthetics and composition. However, the techniques are not merely aesthetic tools to be universally applied. We are suggesting a slightly different approach to their use, namely that these grouping techniques be emphasized in the overall design concept for those clients who demonstrate a strong need for order in the interview. At a minimum, rooms should be designed and furnishings should be arranged to conform with people's natural grouping tendencies. On the other hand, the client may place more of an emphasis on variety (see Chapter 7) than on order. In this case, we should avoid a look that is too ordered and structured and, instead, depend more on the design concepts discussed in Chapter 7.

Figure-ground contrast

Instead of perceiving the environment in a homogeneous manner we see figures against an amorphous background. Sharpe (1975) devotes an entire chapter to a discussion of how color and pattern reinforce the differentiation between figure and ground. We will mention several of her design suggestions and make a few recommendations of our own.

We think that people with a need for order have a strong preference for clear, distinct, and stable figure-ground combinations. Therefore, in the beginning stages of room planning for these individuals, designers should decide upon which features will be figure and which will be background, and should do whatever is possible to enhance the contrast between these elements.

In the perception of a room, furniture is usually seen as figure against a background of walls and floors. This tendency can be reinforced by using upholstery with distinct patterns or bright colors while keeping the background neutral.

If it is decided that both the furniture and the floor covering are to be light, the floor covering should be limited to the area occupied by the furniture so that this area, as figure, can be contrasted from the remainder of the room. Generally, we wouldn't recommend monochromatic color schemes for large areas of space when creating an environment for a person with a strong need for order; figure-ground contrast would be insufficient. However, if client preferences, or other considerations, dictate the use of a monochromatic arrangement, the furniture should be spaced widely apart so that one can see around and between pieces.

Other room features, such as walls used for the display of art objects, paintings, elaborate wall coverings, and window treatments, can function as the figure. Prior experience, values, and needs also determine what is perceived most prominently, so that a room can be organized around a treasured object or valued piece of furniture. In any case, we wouldn't want to have too many things in a room competing for the attention of a person with a strong order-need. A room with too many figures would appear cluttered and disorganized, and would disrupt figure-ground perception.

Spatial separation

As the distance between room elements decreases, the tendency to see them as members of a common grouop increases. Designers should take advantage of this perceptual phenomenon, known as the "law of proximity," in order to design orderly environments. Groupings of objects, furniture, etc. should be emphasized, with small distances between group elements and larger distances between separate groups. Distinct areas can also be bounded by partitions, screens, and other symbolic devices to aid further in the perceptual organization of the room (see Chapter 2: Control of Space/ Territoriality).

Continuity

If the spatial separation techniques discussed in the last section are to be used successfully, the elements of the various groups or areas should relate to each other in some fashion. The room should not appear too complex or too fragmented. Unity must be achieved.

According to the "law of similarity," we perceive wholes out of parts that are similar in color, brightness, pattern, shape, size, texture, etc. We also perceive unities on the basis of shared meanings. In other words, elements may differ in form but may express a common theme (for example, a style or an activity). For example, a room may consist of functionally distinct sections; but if these areas represent the varied activities of a family, the room can still be perceived as a unit on the basis of similarity of meaning. This perception can be enhanced by the subtle repetition of color and other symbolic techniques.

Of course, we are not saying anything that is drastically different from what the experienced designer does in creating a design concept that flows and holds together in aesthetics and composition. We are saying, however, that achieving continuity should be the focus of design activities when dealing with clients whose need for perceptual order dominates.

Balance

Clients with a strong need for order seem to prefer balanced designs, as the following comments suggest:

The fact that we have not been able to get everything in its proper place is rather unsettling.

The furniture and space were harmonious.

I like things to match—a balanced look is appealing to me.

For these individuals, we recommend an emphasis upon symmetry in design, with particular attention to the perception of colors and forms. The following represents a partial list of some familiar techniques to accomplish this goal: a composition in which horizontal and vertical lines predominate; traditional arrangements of the more formal period styles; stability, balance, and serenity in contemporary furnishings; a balance of opposites (for example, warm and cool colors or large and small objects); controlled variety (for example, repetition of lines and forms).

As a general rule, the dynamic movement created by strong diagonal lines should be avoided. However, rooms can be diagonally balanced by having the major portion of open space confined to the upper-right corner in relation to the entrance and by placing bulky elements in the lower-left corner. This observation is based upon Cunningham's (1977) study of right- and left-oriented apartment floor plans. In this experiment, subjects preferred to have living rooms, the largest area in the plan, located in the far right-hand corner of the apartment rather than in the far left-hand corner. This result agrees with a similar right-left asymmetry in judging the aesthetic balance of paintings; that is, the upper right-hand corner of a picture should contain more empty volume than the upper left-hand corner to balance out the additional weight that the lower left-hand corner is capable of carrying (Arnheim, 1954). What may be true of paintings and floor plans may also be true of room layouts.

Clarity

According to S. Kaplan (1975), humans depend heavily upon their information-processing skills in order to adapt successfully to the environment. Environments that are easy to comprehend are, therefore, highly preferred. We like landscapes that are identifiable (S. Kaplan, 1975), cities that are legible (Lynch, 1960), and social situations in which the rules for behavior are clear (Moos, 1976).

Clarity is an important determinant of environmental preference for novel, unfamiliar, and complex places. However, people with a strong need for order may also demand that the more familiar home environment be particularly clear and legible.

Conventional design elements

In one sense, a concern for clarity may lead to a preference for product names with which clients are familiar through advertising. If the interview reveals that order is a high-priority need, we can suggest well-known manufacturers for furniture, fabrics, wallpaper, floor coverings, lighting, fixtures, etc. If other products in the same line are of higher quality, this fact can be pointed out so that the client can make a choice. If order is a predominant need, the identifiability of a particular name may outweigh aesthetic considerations. In any case, a preference test, where one choice is pitted against another, will reinforce the interpretation of which client needs are dominant over others.

Things should also appear to be what they really are. A chair should look like a chair; a bed should look like a bed. An object which appears to be out of context, such as a ceramic lamp shaped like a woman's hat, may serve the need for variety but may be disorienting to a person who prefers an orderly, predictable environment. And, novelty for its own sake, unless carefully done, has never been considered of great aesthetic value.

Similarly, we should be careful about the use of simulations (for example, laminated plastics that look like wood for butcher-block work surfaces in kitchens). The problem with these substitutions is that our expectations are violated. We expect the feel of wood, but instead we get the feel of plastic. Eventually we will adapt, probably by changing our expectations. But in the meantime, we are annoyed, temporarily confused, and even threatened by our inability to make accurate predictions about the environment.

And it's becoming increasingly difficult to tell what things really are as more accurate simulations are devised (for example, spraying vinyl made to look like leather with a substance that also makes it smell like leather). The following humorous account illustrates the confusion that this trend is causing:

> *I have been so confused lately. Recently I bought a pair of shoes that had the look of vinyl simulating leather. When I spilled something on one, I decided to try and cover it with shoe polish. Normally you can't do this with vinyl, but I thought there was an outside chance that there were manufactured pores built into the vinyl. I was totally mixed up when it worked so well that I called the store to double check. (No information was given to me at the time of purchase.) Then, I found out that the shoes were indeed leather even though they neither looked nor smelled like leather. So now leather doesn't always look or smell like leather and vinyl does.*

The preceding example had to do with shoes. But vinyl and leather are also used for upholstery. What if a cleaning person uses a household cleaner recommended for vinyl on a leather chair by mistake?

There are times, however, when simulations represent an appropriate design solution. In one case, we used fabricated greens to conceal the unfinished top of a storage unit, which could have been seen from a balcony and staircase. Real plants would have died in that location for a number of reasons.

Some designers may object to the use of simulations on purely aesthetic grounds, regarding such things as the hat lamp or the artificial plants as being "tacky" or in "poor taste." We have been emphasizing the importance of authenticity from a different perspective (for instance, the importance of environmental clarity). However, design issues can become rather complex when needs come into conflict with each other. Clarity may not always be aesthetically pleasing.

Again, we think that these problems can be resolved by giving clients information about the relationship between design and need-satisfaction. If they are informed, in this manner, about choices and potential outcomes, clients can then make decisions on the basis of which needs are dominant. Need will naturally dictate preference.

Here's an example of what we mean. Let's assume that a decision is being made with respect to kitchen counter tops. We can then provide clients with the following information about the alternatives: Simulated butcher block has decorative appeal, is easy to maintain, but lacks clarity; wood butcher block may be aesthetically pleasing and legible (for instance, we know what it is), but is difficult to maintain; plastic laminates that do not have the look of wood are easy to maintain, and don't pretend to be what they are not, but may not be as pleasing in a visual sense.

If we proceed in this manner, clients will know what to expect. The need for clarity will be served no matter what choice is made.

Perceptual clarity

The quality of lighting in a room directly affects the perception of form, color, space, etc. Because clients with a strong need for order may be particularly concerned with perceptual clarity, we recommend the use of lighting arrangements that result in bright, clear, and distinct images.

The field of lighting technology is advancing at a rapid rate. It is beyond the scope of this book to summarize the latest developments; therefore, we will make no specific recommendations in this area. We expect the competent design professional to have at least a general working knowledge of this technology and to consult with a lighting specialist if necessary in particular cases.

In addition to making lighting recommendations, sources of visual distortion or disorientation should also be eliminated. One of our subjects mentioned such a problem:

> *One area of the house that used to bother me was the bathroom floor. It was made of many small black and white tiles which all but blinded you in the middle of the night.*

Some other things to avoid are as follows: vertical stripes in wall coverings, which may appear distorted because of their color combinations; three-dimensional effects in carpet, tile, or highly polished floors, which may interfere with depth perception in the aging eye; glare from chrome, specular walls, and furnishings, which may be a particular problem for older persons; and any designed space that deviates drastically from the expected (for example, carpet on the ceiling).

Household Maintenance

In the last section, we emphasized the significance of the way things look to people. Here we are more concerned with function.

For a large number of our subjects, order was closely associated with the maintenance of the home. These individuals placed quite a bit of importance upon neatness, cleanliness, accessibility, convenience, and practicality. The following subject captures a number of these maintenance dimensions in the description of her kitchen: "My kitchen/dining area now is ultra-modern and streamlined; I love it for its conveniences, clean look, and workability."

Cleanliness

Generally speaking, designers should use their knowledge of maintenance-free and easy-to-care-for products, materials, surfaces, etc. to assist clients in keeping the home neat and clean with a minimum of effort. Here is a partial list of design alternatives:

1. Finishes, weaves, hues, and patterns that don't readily show wear or dirt (for example, mat finishes, tight-weave carpeting, complex patterns for floors and fabrics, and middle-toned hues).

2. Techniques to protect surfaces and materials (for example, a blotter or a fitted piece of glass for wood desk surfaces, a polyurethane coating for wood, a soil-repellent coating for fabrics, and a static resistant treatment for synthetic yarns).

3. Self-cleaning appliances.

4. Easy-to-clean surfaces and areas (for example, fiberglass instead of tiles in the bath, seamless resilient floors, and easy-to-disassemble diffusers on fixtures).

5. Products with replaceable parts (for example, a patio chair that can be restrung).

6. Devices to hide trash from view.

Additionally, in planning furniture arrangements and room layouts, hard-to-vacuum places and hard-to-reach surfaces should be avoided. Sommer (1974) found that in public environments (for example, schools) furniture arrangements are primarily determined by maintenance staff rather than by teachers and students. In the home, the people who are using the environment may be the same ones who clean it. They should, therefore, be made aware of how room arrangement affects both the ease of maintenance and the activities that occur in that space. Then, some meaningful compromise can be effected between the two.

Orderly Use of Space

You probably won't be surprised to learn that many of our subjects mentioned the need for additional space in the home. But what accounts for this desire? For one thing, adequate space is needed to maintain an orderly environment. Looked at from the opposite perspective, spatial inadequacy may produce the cluttered and confusing environment that people with a strong order-need find so aversive. Although we may not always be able to increase the amount of available space for clients, we can at least help them use space wisely, so that they can store their things neatly, retrieve them easily, and use them conveniently.

Storage

First of all, it's important to understand the organizational function that storage performs for us. The following interviews illustrate this point very well:

I use my big closet and my drawers to organize clothes, shoes, and suitcases.

I would like a room with a lot of closet and storage space. I feel very disorganized when I don't have a lot of storage.

So when people are asking for additional floor space, closets, shelves, drawers, containers, etc., they are really expressing a desire for order and organization in their lives.

In order to help clients fulfill this need, we can pay attention to the spatial references made in the interview. Many times, a variety of storage problems will be revealed. For example, one subject mentioned that she had no place to put keys, books, etc. in the entryway, no cabinet underneath the bathroom sink to provide extra shelving space, and insufficient drawer space in the bedroom. These problems can be solved with either available products or created ones, utilizing space-saving techniques (for example, walls and ceilings for hanging utensils and other objects), multifunctional design elements (for example, a bookcase that also functions as a space divider), built-ins, and other familiar methods. Information can also be more conveniently stored on computer diskettes than in written form, with the added advantage of rapid retrieval.

In order to solve the common problem of insufficient closet space, a small nonessential room or a room that might be ordinarily used for another purpose (for example, a den, a spare room, or a sewing room) can be remodeled into a highly practical and organized closet. The spaciousness of such an arrangement would greatly facilitate organization; and if things got a little out of order, the door can always be shut. Although, in some cases, this technique may result in sacrificing space that could be used for other functions, the trade-off may be well worth it for people with a strong order-need.

Storage space can also be created in a large room by concealing the to-be-stored items behind decorative sliding panels on tracks. Children's games and toys are hidden from view in this manner and are still readily available for play.

Access

Using space wisely means much more than just having places to put things away. If we are to use these things, we must know where they are and be able to get at them with a minimum of effort.

First of all, let's talk about the relationship between storage, memory, and retrieval. It's very easy for us to use spatial cues to help us remember things. Thomas (1977) even thinks that the tendency to associate memory with place is inherited. In any case, having differentiated storage space helps us keep track of where things are.

Different items can be placed in particular locations. Storage areas can be appropriately sectioned. The distinctiveness of these spaces can be enhanced by color coding, labeling, etc. All of the preceding techniques would help people avoid memory retrieval problems like the one reported by the following person:

Sometimes it's too much effort to put my clothes away. They usually end up on the floor, on the bed, or somewhere else. Later I have a hard time remembering exactly where I left them.

Other people may prefer to have visual access to their possessions instead of having to remember what they own and where they are keeping it. This is probably the reason that one of our subjects said that "full and complete viewing of my clothes without a drawer in sight is a must."

The "closet-room" that we suggested earlier would probably work well for this subject (and others like her). She could walk into the room, visually review her wardrobe, and perhaps even have enough space to dress there.

You may have noticed that while we were discussing memory problems, we also referred to the issue of effort in retrieval. Most of us seem to work according to a least-effort principle. If access to a particular item is too difficult, we may choose not to use it, as the following personal account illustrates:

I keep a collection of my favorite books stacked one on top of another on a series of wall shelves in my bedroom. I use the rest of the shelf space for displaying my other possessions. It's nice to see my books stacked neatly there, but I never seem to read them anymore. I guess it's too much trouble.

The book-storage system used in the preceding example failed to take into account the need to minimize effort in the retrieving of things. A horizontal arrangement, rather than a vertical one, would have provided a better compromise between storage and access. Items that are rarely used can be stacked in order to save space; but for regularly used items, "use files not piles."

Accessibility can also be increased by having things within one's reach. One of our subjects described her kitchen, which was designed in this manner:

The kitchen is done in navy and white with antiques and pottery wherever I can hang it. Everything is easily accessible. All my utensils are out at my fingertips, and pots and pans can be pulled out in a second's notice.

Great care should be taken in designing the kitchen for clients who, like the previous individual, emphasize order/accessibility issues in the interview. Thoughtful consideration should be given to the selection of design elements that increase access (for example, kitchen cabinets that are accessible to people of different sizes, ladders on rollers for hard-to-reach areas, and transistorized appliances that take up little counter space), without sacrificing aesthetics.

Designers may have to decide between designs that emphasize neat storage and designs that stress accessibility because some people may prefer the former, and other people may prefer the latter. Weisner and Weibel (1981) found two such opposite tendencies in their survey of family life styles in California. In conventional homes, things were cleared away, were stored in containers, and were out of sight. On the other hand, nonconventional homes seemed to place more emphasis upon "easy access to ongoing activities." The interview, with additional probes if necessary, should provide some information about which of these categories the client falls into.

Alternatively, it may be possible to strike a compromise between the neat, clean, cleared-away look and the accessibility factor. This can be accomplished in several ways. Things can be "at one's fingertips" (remember the kitchen we described earlier) but well integrated in the total design of the area. Or accessible storage spaces can minimize effort in both storing and retrieving objects.

To expand on the second point, many people don't put things away because it's too much trouble to do so: "When it's too much trouble to put something away, I usually just throw it on the floor." Now if we could make it easy to put something away and have it located close to where it is used, the problem may be solved. The concealed storage space behind sliding panels may be an example of such a solution.

Finally, the physical limitations of children and special populations such as the elderly, the disabled, and the infirm may make accessibility a high-priority design issue. A discussion of such problems, along with some suggested solutions and appropriate references, can be found in Chapter 4: Self-Evaluation/Environmental Control.

Organization of Activities

At the beginning of the chapter, we defined order as a preference for neat and organized environments. The design concepts that we have discussed so far have followed this definition by emphasizing external concerns (for example, balance, symmetry, and cleanliness). However, people also like to maintain a kind of internal order. They like to see themselves as organized individuals who can think and plan clearly, and work efficiently.

There are a number of environmental properties that help people achieve behavioral organization during work, study, or leisure activities. We would like to make you aware of some of them, but we will not attempt to generate an exhaustive list of the environmental requirements for various behaviors. Nor will we attempt to discuss the complicated issues involved in the increased use of home offices; Becker (1981), in the last chapter of *Workspace* does an excellent job of that. Instead, we will concentrate on variables, primarily spatial ones, that are most closely associated with achieving order in both work and play.

Territoriality

Because territoriality functions in a number of ways to promote the organization of behavior (Edney, 1976), ideally, household members should have separate spaces in the home for their work. Obviously, it's necessary to have a place to stay when engaged in thought and action over long periods of time. And we certainly need a place to store and use any required equipment. But beyond that, familiar surroundings minimize distraction and, therefore, help us concentrate and think clearly. And if we continually use this place for sustained work, the environment itself becomes a stimulus for our work, motivating us to get started and to persist until the job is done. As we have argued throughout this book, territoriality also helps us achieve environmental control. So when we occupy our work place, we can choose our activity freely and successfully resist potential interruptions.

Of course, we have been speaking about the ideal case. It's not always possible to provide isolated work locations in the home for those household members who need them. In the absence of sufficient space, the boundary suggestions discussed in Chapter 2 can at least provide some of the advantages of separate territories. However, for these "weak territories" to work, household members will have to learn adaptive strategies that facilitate close cooperation and coordination of behavior. The designer can only do so much.

Surface Space

As a general rule, designers should attempt to maximize the amount of usable surface space for the client's chosen activities. Let's look at several interviews to understand why.

My desk was oversized, and I loved to spread my papers and drawings all over but within easy reach.

"Spreading out" allows us to take over a space and surround ourselves with our work. Then we can really concentrate on what we are doing and be totally involved in it.

Spreading out also implies spaciousness. There is sufficient room to keep our things in order. Under these conditions, we can approach our task in an organized manner, slow down, and enjoy ourselves. We may also be able to think more clearly as the following personal account suggests:

When I play cards, I need a large table to have room for the cards, discards, scoring sheets, etc. I need space to keep things neat and organized so I can concentrate on the game, think clearly, and make good decisions about strategy.

Surface space should not only be large, it should also be differentiated to provide for a variety of functions. Space is needed for the main work area and for equipment and supplies. It is also desirable to have a place for work in progress to stand. When we are working on a project over an extended period of time, we like to keep our things out. The trouble that it takes to put things away and take them out again may interfere with work, whereas the sight of ongoing work may even motivate us to come back to it. But space should be designed and/or arranged so that work in progress is hidden from the view of others in order to maintain privacy and a look of order. At times we may be working on several jobs at once. Again it would be undesirable to put one job away in order to work on the other. Instead, surface space should be expandable to accommodate concurrent activities.

With respect to other factors that contribute to efficient, comfortable work-space furnishings and configurations, designers can refer to the latest available information on office design and use whatever is appropriate for the home work area.

Storage and Access

As we emphasized in the section on the orderly use of space, convenient access to supplies, materials, etc. is a high priority item. Thus, Seal and Sylvester (1982) found that many members of their sample of office workers preferred a close relationship between storage space and work space. One way to achieve this relationship is by providing overhead shelving in close proximity to the work surface area, a specific request made by 42 percent of the employees interviewed by the aforementioned authors.

We would also like to repeat several of our earlier recommendations because they are particularly applicable in this context. For one thing, the availability of differentiated storage spaces (for example, separate locations for current work, reference materials, supplies, etc.) helps us organize our activities. Second, the computer can also perform an important organizational function for clients like the following: "I like electronic equipment and feel excited about the possibilities of using computers to organize my business life."

This last interview suggests that designers should be aware of the environmental conditions that affect work with computers. The Seal and Sylvester article, mentioned earlier, contains a number of design recommendations for software employees in offices, which can also be applied to the home. And the latest in computer furniture and other accessories is often advertised in trade magazines.

In a more general sense, the layout of a room should be organized around the important tasks that occur there. These activities, whether work-related or not, can then be performed in an orderly fashion. Designers should pay attention to what clients say about storage, access, convenience, etc. in order to understand which room arrangements are working well and which ones are unsatisfactory.

One member of our sample described how access to certain activities is maintained by the layout of the living room:

> *The stereo and television are in convenient and practical locations. The buffet that holds all the china, crystal, and silverware is convenient to the dining room and the kitchen.*

If we were working on other aspects of this room, we would take care that these relationships are not disturbed. On the other hand, clients may pinpoint specific areas for intervention by mentioning problems like the following one:

> *We keep our new freezer in the basement. However, it's a lot of trouble to reach the food because of all the other junk piled around it. It's also a pain to run up and down the steps from the kitchen to the basement all the time.*

Displays

Two types of verbal displays can be used as organizers and motivators of work and other creative activities: a favorite saying, proverb, or individualized message to express the meaning of the activity and a calendar, note pad, or message board to act as a prompt, reminding people of important task-related details. In order for these displays to be maximally effective as prompts, they should be located in the work area, next to the place where the prompted behavior is to occur (Delprato, 1977).

People may also require a place to exhibit completed work (for example, art, photographs, etc.). This type of display can motivate people to persevere when they experience inevitable setbacks. Therefore, these successes should be in full view of the work area but should also be oriented so as to screen this private area from the view of others.

Privacy

Certainly privacy is essential for organized thought and action. We have just mentioned how completed work can be used as a display and as a visual screen. Other techniques for achieving both visual and acoustic privacy can be found in Chapter 3. Designs from this chapter that minimize interference from others are also relevant here. We have already advocated the use of separate territories—space permitting—as a physical separation technique.

Other Environmental Conditions

We have mentioned a number of design variables which, we think, are most closely associated with the organization of behavior. In order to design successful work spaces, a number of additional environmental conditions must be considered. These factors, which seem to be particularly important to people when shortcomings exist (Farrenkopf and Roth, 1980), include proper furnishings, heating, ventilation, air conditioning, and lighting (see Chapter 2) as well as windows, views, and other aesthetic considerations (see Chapter 8).

VARIETY

— 7 —

A number of psychologists have argued that people tend to seek out and prefer different levels of stimulation (for example, Fiske and Maddi, 1961; Mehrabian and Russell, 1973; Zuckerman et al., 1964). Some people feel comfortable when they are aroused, activated, stimulated, and excited; a relatively high state of arousal is natural for them. Others feel more comfortable in a low arousal state, when there is less internal and external stimulation present.

Although differences between people in this need for stimulation have been identified, it is also important to remember that differences exist within the person at different times. We have all experienced occasions when we are understimulated and, consequently, have a need for variety, novelty, and change. And, at other times, we may be overstimulated so that we prefer conditions of sameness, calm, and quiet.

Designers should be aware of this important dimension of personality so that they are able to design interiors that help people achieve an optimal level of arousal at a particular point in time. The design concepts discussed in this chapter should be of assistance in achieving this goal. First of all, we will describe how environments can be created to facilitate stimulation seeking. Then we will illustrate how to design places for people who wish to reduce stimulation.

The client interview should be helpful in determining whether a high or a low need for stimulation exists. Interview examples mentioned in the sections to follow are meant to illustrate the kinds of things that high need and low need individuals say. Then, depending upon the analysis of the client's average arousal level, concepts from either the stimulation-seeking

98

or the stimulation-reducing sections can be emphasized in the overall design of the home. However, designers should be prepared to design for a range of arousal levels around this average because a person's level of arousal changes from time to time. This goal can be accomplished by creating separate high stimulation and low stimulation areas or by creating flexible spaces in which the overall level of arousal can be easily altered.

Stimulation Seeking

When our current level of arousal is below our preferred level, a need for stimulation exists. We will then attempt to seek out and/or produce stimulation in order to raise arousal to a level that is normal and comfortable for us. Stimulation seeking, however, can take on a number of different forms; we have choices as to how to satisfy the need for stimulation. In the sections to follow, a series of design concepts are described for each of three different varieties of stimulation seeking: environmental stimulation, learning, and creative thought. These alternative methods of increasing arousal were inspired by Pearson's (1970) forms of novelty experiencing.

Environmental Stimulation

One way to satisfy the need for stimulation is to seek out environments that have a high stimulation value (for instance, places or situations that are unusual, complex, exciting, etc.). Although we would expect people to go outside the home to satisfy this need, by engaging in activities such as travel and outdoor sports, stimulation seekers also prefer home environments that are involving and interesting. The design concepts discussed below are essentially attributes of the home environment that contribute to its stimulation value.

Complexity

Complexity refers to the number and diversity of elements in an environment. The following home descriptions fit this definition and represent preferred interiors for people in need of stimulation:

> *I spent long hours studying a panel of stained glass windows. . . .*
> *Each one was slightly different from the next, and I would play*
> *games with myself finding the differences.*

> *My home is eclectic, made up of my travels through the many*
> *trips I've taken. It is a home of many facets and directions.*

Below we have listed a number of ways of achieving complexity in the home environment. However, if these concepts are to be applied correctly, remember that people generally prefer environments with intermediate degrees of stimulation, places that provide some diversity but not so much as to confuse, bewilder, and disorient (S. Kaplan, 1975). This outcome can be achieved by unifying complex elements within an overall pattern, as Rapoport and Kantor (1976) have suggested. Such designs would simultaneously satisfy both the need for stimulation and the need for order. We will have more to say about the interaction between variety and order when we discuss more specific design suggestions in this chapter and when we present alternate approaches to environmental aesthetics in the next chapter.

Decorative complexity.   Weisner and Weibel (1981) found that both conventional and nonconventional homes differ according to a decorative complexity factor. Complex interiors contain such characteristics as a variety of objects (for example, antiques, collections, floor pillows, books, plants, and flower arrangements), a large amount of wall decoration (for example, arrangements of prints and photographs, maps, posters, and wall hangings), and an eclectic mix of styles. The "eclectic" home "of many facets and directions" that we previously mentioned fits in well here.

Detail.   Interiors designed with attention to detail tend to provide a rich variety of external stimulation, increase visual exploration, and, therefore, maintain arousal. (Recall the subject who spent much time trying to differentiate between the various stained glass panels.) Detail can also be achieved with trim (for example, fringe and tassels on window treatments, cornices, and valances), pattern (for example, in fabrics, carpets, tile floors, and wall coverings), and other forms of ornamentation (for example, carved frames for furnishings, detailed hardware for doors and cabinets, ornamental friezes, and structural beams).

Light and color.   The use of a variety of interior colors increases the visual complexity of the home. However, if a monochromatic color scheme is more appropriate for the space being designed, it is best to choose a color that has a wide range of possible variations in value, such as red, blue, green, or violet.

Visual variety can also be created with lighting. Maximum use should be made of lighting techniques for vertical surfaces, such as wall washing, wall grazing, pools of light created by recessed downlighting, and projections of pictures and patterns. Because both laboratory studies (for example, Flynn et al., 1973) and our own experience indicate that people find complex lighting arrangements more interesting than simple ones, we recommend the use of a variety of lighting systems within a space (for example, ambient light combined with decorative and task lamps). Finally, we can also take advantage of light and shadow effects (for example, indirect lighting of mobile sculptures and uplighting of plants).

Spatial complexity.   Eliovson (1978) describes how a Japanese garden, divided into portions by screens, fences, trees, and rocks, can invite exploration. Interiors that are spatially differentiated can have the same effect on us. A home divided by walls into a number of small rooms, or a room divided into distinct areas with appropriate boundaries (see Chapter 2: Control of Space/Territoriality), provides more environmental stimulation than a more homogeneous arrangement of space. However, don't forget Rapoport and Kantor (1976); spatial complexity without unity can be disquieting rather than appealing. In Chapter 6: Perceptual Organization/Continuity, some ideas are presented for balancing these two attributes.

Density.   Generally speaking, densely furnished rooms provide us with more varied stimulation than sparsely furnished ones. Therefore, it would be appropriate to select styles that lend themselves well to having many furnishings in a relatively small area. Density can also be created by applying the Japanese practice of miniaturization in art and gardening (Altman, 1975) to the design of interiors; that is, rooms can be filled with a variety of objects that are small in scale.

Additionally, Mehrabian and Russell (1974b) point out that high densities are associated with small distances between people and other elements of a room. Under these conditions, object details become more apparent as sources of stimulation. Therefore, the stimulation value of art work, collections, accessories, etc. can be enhanced by creating room arrangements that permit up-close viewing of these objects.

Furthermore, densely furnished rooms reduce distances between people, who are also sources of varied stimulation. Care must be taken, however, to assure that these close interaction distances are experienced positively; a condition of crowding should not be created.

We will say much more about this problem in Chapter 10 as we discuss the satisfaction of social needs. For now a simple example will suffice. A sofa, no matter how long it is, may not comfortably accommodate more than two individuals unless people are engaged in some distracting activity or are members of a common group. Alternatively, an arrangement of separate chairs provides each person with some territorial control as well as the stimulation of the close presence of others. The latter arrangement should also allow people to vary eye contact more comfortably, particularly if corner-to-corner seating is employed.

Personalization.   In Chapter 4 we learned that people personalize their homes to aid in the process of self-definition. Personalizing the living environment also increases its complexity (Becker and Coniglio, 1975). Therefore, the personalization categories and techniques developed in Chapter 4 can be quite helpful to designers as their application may result in the satisfaction of both the need for identity and the need for stimulation.

Functional complexity.   Weisner and Weibel (1981) characterized some homes as being high in functional complexity. In these homes, space is used in highly creative and flexible ways to reinforce an "organic" life style. Rather than having different rooms serve different functions, a variety of activities may take place in a single area. Greater importance is placed upon creating a lived-in feeling and having ready access to ongoing activities than upon maintaining order, neatness, and cleanliness.

Some research suggests that a functionally complex interior may appeal to the stimulation seeker. For example, Samuelson and Lindauer (1976) found that people with a high need for stimulation preferred the diversity of a messy room to the simplicity of a neat room. Both rooms contained the same items; but in the messy room, objects and papers were scattered about on a table rather than being put away and neatly stacked, suggesting the comfortable accessibility of Weisner and Weibel's functionally complex homes.

Now we certainly are not suggesting that designers create messy and disorderly interiors as a way of increasing environmental stimulation. Instead, functional complexity can be built into a room in an aesthetically pleasing manner, with the liberal use of soft architecture, multifunctional furniture, and territorial zoning (see Chapter 2).

Change and evolution.   The previously discussed concepts for increasing environmental complexity may satisfy the need for stimulation, but for how long? People may adapt to, and become bored with, even high-complexity home interiors because of continual exposure to them. One of our subjects discussed this problem thusly:

> *One behavior that I perform frequently is constantly rearranging the furniture in my room. I am unable to stand keeping my room the same. I believe this is because I spend so much of my time in my room; and, therefore, I get tired of it quickly. I usually change my furniture around about every six to eight weeks.*

The preceding interview seems to be suggesting that the possibility of change may counteract the familiarity of the home environment. We concur. Homes should be temporally complex, capable of being changed over time. Design should encourage both change and evolution, and invite the person to participate in these processes. As one subject said, "My future home would be a long-term design project with the possibility for change."

Think of interior space as a painting which, as a work of art, is never finished. The artist may do many versions of the same theme as people may re-arrange the elements of a room. The artist may be continually adding the extra brush stroke after being away from the painting for a while. In the same way, collections may evolve, detailing may be added to minimalist contemporary settings, etc.

The section on underdesigned space in Chapter 2 provides some additional ideas for creating interiors that support change. The input of a designer is particularly important here to make sure that these "unfinished" rooms are aesthetically pleasing at all stages of development and/or transformation.

Intensity

Some stimuli have more of an effect upon our level of arousal than others. We respond more to a strong stimulus (for example, a bright light) than to a weak one. We are attracted to places and situations that are characterized by a high degree of sensory involvement. And highly meaningful, emotionally significant stimuli can have a substantial impact upon us.

Vividness.   Vivid visual experiences (for example, striking patterns and bold designs) can increase the stimulation value of the home. Lighting and color are extremely important in this regard. Brightly lit rooms are more stimulating than dimly lit ones (Mehrabian, 1976). With regard to color, the warm end of the spectrum (red, orange, and yellow) is generally associated with excitement and stimulation (Sharpe, 1975). Darker and more saturated colors from this end of the spectrum (for example, a dark, deep red) are also more arousing than brighter and less saturated ones (Mehrabian and Russell, 1974a).

Sensory involvement.   A room that appeals to different sensory modalities is much more involving than one that provides only visual experiences. In Chapter 4 we mentioned that rooms associated with characteristic sounds, odors, and textures facilitate attachment to place (see Attachment/ Vivid Sensory Experiences). These same techniques can also be employed to satisfy the need for stimulation.

Fabrics and materials can be selected for their ability to encourage active involvement with the environment through touch, providing smooth (polished wood and stainless steel), soft (velvet and fur), and/or rough (tweed and wool) sensations. Some of these same materials also appeal to the temperature sense, giving us an experience of coldness (metals) or warmth (woods). Kinetic experiences are particularly involving; we love things such as chairs and beds that massage and vibrate as well as swings, rockers, etc. that allow us to experience motion. See the next chapter, on aesthetics, for some additional ways of appealing to the senses.

Emotional impact.   Things in the environment can have stimulation value because of the way they affect us emotionally. We may react strongly to a painting, a piece of sculpture, an awe-inspiring view, or even a flower. Other objects or themes may have a deep emotional meaning for us because of their association with our personal past. The client interview should be helpful in identifying those things that evoke strong emotional reactions. Look for emotionally laden language such as: "I have warm feelings about, I was overwhelmed by, It was fascinating to."

Unpredictability

In Chapter 6 we discussed the need for people to perceive the environment in an orderly and organized fashion. However, when there is too much patterning, regularity, and redundancy, we tend to get bored and uninvolved. Certainly we want the home environment to be a predictable one, so that the needs for order and security are satisfied. But if homes are designed with some degree of surprise, unexpectedness, and uncertainty, we can serve the need for stimulation as well.

Motion. Things that move are more unpredictable, and are therefore more stimulating, than static objects. There are a variety of ways of incorporating motion into interior design including projected images, mobiles, kinetic sculpture, and mechanical novelties. For example, we have used a clock with back-lit color gels which, as they turn and cross each other, create a continually changing pattern of color. Moving shadows, produced by indirect lighting of mobile sculptures, and uplighting of plants combined with directed air currents also capture our attention.

Because living things (for example, fish, birds, and other pets) also provide an excellent source of unpredictable stimulation that can keep us occupied, interested, and involved for long periods of time, we should not overlook them as interior design elements. The following subject illustrates this point very well:

> *One of my favorite aspects of my room is my fish tank. I often spend hours watching my fish swimming around and around in the tank. I would like to have a huge fish tank in the living room of my ideal future home.*

Asymmetry. In Japanese gardens, interest is created by selecting and pruning trees with asymmetrical characteristics (for example, the twisting branches of the Japanese maple), by placing a tree "in a strong position" toward the side rather than in the center, and by grouping large and small plants together (Eliovson, 1978).

We can utilize a similar strategy in the composition of a room with design elements and arrangements that are unexpected—but not random, haphazard, and chaotic. The following is a partial list of such techniques:

1. Nature as a source of asymmetry.

2. Soft architectural elements (for example, an assortment of area rugs, pillows, and cushions of all shapes and sizes), all of which would be coordinated in color and pattern to look pleasing no matter how the elements are arranged.

3. Different levels in a room.

4. Diagonal lines with masses of forms.

5. Asymmetrical elements added to orderly, balanced rooms (for example, off-center paintings, asymmetrical arrangements of books and collections, and absence of pairs of furnishings).

You may recall that in Chapter 6 we gave a series of suggestions for creating balance and symmetry as a way of satisfying the need for order. It may appear to you that our current recommendations contradict our earlier ones. In a sense they do because the needs for stimulation and order seem to be in direct opposition to each other (for instance, a high need for stimulation tends to be associated with a low need for order and vice versa). Therefore, designers should make a judgment from the client interview as to which need predominates and proceed accordingly. In the absence of this information, we should attempt to create a healthy balance between regularity and irregularity, order and disorder, symmetry and asymmetry.

Mystery.   S. Kaplan (1975) has found that outdoor scenes in which certain elements are partially hidden from view tend to be very interesting and involving to us. An element of mystery and uncertainty is created by a path that disappears into the horizon or a large tree in the foreground that partially obscures what lies beyond.

The following interviews suggested to us that it may be possible to achieve a similar effect in the interior environment:

> *The house that I grew up in as a child, provided unending mystery and discovery. It had a life of its own and invited exploration of numerous nooks, crannies, closets, and passageways.*

> *My present house is ordinary and utilitarian, there are no sudden surprises or quaint corners.*

Perhaps some of the concepts introduced in Chapter 3 as mechanisms for controlling visual output also would add a sense of mystery to the home (for example, visual barriers, room shape, etc.). Things can be hidden behind screens and partitions. People can come upon unexpected corners and alcoves. And mystery can also be created with lighting (for example, a lot of light and shadow, atmospheric lighting, etc.).

One word of caution, however. Mystery is stimulating because information is suggested, but not completely known. What happens when we find out "what lies beyond the bend"? Does the scene lose its mystery and its capacity to increase arousal? Perhaps so. But this technique may remain quite effective for children, who have a great capacity to be fascinated by the unknown, and for guests, who have yet to explore the client's home.

Ambiguity. Things that lack complete clarity and identifiability may be stimulating to the imagination. Thus, the stimulation seeker may be intrigued by abstract art and sculpture (for example, expressionism, cubism, and surrealism). However, this technique should be used in moderation as S. Kaplan argues that people also may react with anger and hostility to ambiguous stimuli (see Chapter 6: Perceptual Organization/Clarity).

Scale. Mehrabian and Russell (1974) point out that familiar objects experienced at a larger-than-normal scale (for example, as in pop art) can have at least a temporary emotional impact upon us because of their unexpectedness. Stimulation seekers may, in fact, like large-scale design elements for that reason, but others may be shocked, jolted, and intimidated by them. On the other hand, objects experienced at a smaller-than-normal scale may be equally as unexpected and as stimulating, but probably are not as jolting to the senses. Child-size copies of antiques, collections of objects for doll houses or display, etc. may, therefore, satisfy the stimulation needs of a wider range of people.

Contrast. People are continually making comparisons between environmental stimuli as they search for similarities and meaningful groupings that provide continuity to their experience of the world. But people also look for differences in stimulation that provide an unexpected, but welcome, departure from the monotony of sameness, similarity, and homogeneity. Strong contrasts in color and style (for example, a room "furnished traditionally with antiques thrown in for a change of pace," as one subject said) may satisfy this need.

Novelty

We tend to seek out novel environments, which contain elements that are beyond the range of our past experiences, in order to satisfy the need for stimulation. However, by definition, once we have experienced these new stimuli, they tend to lose their novelty and their capacity to stimulate us. After adaptation has occurred, it would appear that we would have to seek out other new places and experiences in order to maintain arousal through novelty. Therefore, in order to apply this concept successfully to the home environment, which is experienced on a day-to-day basis, newness must be combined with other sources of stimulation (for example, meaningfulness and change).

Uniqueness. The home can be furnished with things that are rare, original, and unusual: antiques, art objects, handmade furniture, and craft items. These furnishings and accessories are stimulating initially because of novelty; but even after the novelty has worn off, they may still have the capacity to maintain our interest because of meaningfulness. In other words, these rare and unique pieces can become treasured objects of great meaning and personal significance, particularly if the client is initially involved in their selection and/or creation.

Generally speaking, we would not recommend the use of trendy, faddish home furnishings. These items, like high fashion clothes, can become tiring after the style has worn thin and, thus, can quickly lose their novelty as well as their meaning.

New information about the world. S. Kaplan (1975) maintains that we have survived as a species by depending upon our highly developed ability to process information about the environment. We have already mentioned the importance of making sense of the world in Chapter 6; however, in addition to that, people also enjoy seeking out new information. Consequently, environments that give us the chance to acquire new information are highly valued. And, according to our perspective, these places provide us with opportunities to satisfy the need for stimulation.

The tendency to seek out new information about the world in order to maintain interest is not limited to travel, vacations, etc.; we do the same thing at home. When we look out the window or turn on the radio, we are attempting to establish some connection with the outside world. This form of stimulation seeking is particularly important for those who are house bound (for example, elderly, infirm, handicapped, and parents with young children).

The window is an excellent source of change, variety, and new information as we can directly experience the time, the weather, and other environmental and social events. We love to learn about what is going on around us from the safety of the home.

But what can we do as designers to facilitate this process? For one thing, we can apply some of the design guidelines developed by Verderber (1982) for increasing the "windowness" of therapeutic environments, to the home. In his study, people preferred windows that permitted un-obstructed access to all layers of a view (for instance, ground, buildings, and sky) at once. This result suggests that in new installations, we should use vertical, rather than horizontal, windows. However, as Verderber points out, sills should not be so low that the person feels exposed when looking out; we don't want to give the person a feeling of being "on stage." Casement windows, which can be opened to provide a clear view of the outdoors, may also be a good idea. Additionally, windows can be enlarged to increase access to view layers. And window treatments that destroy the coherence of the view by "dissecting it into many ribbons" (for example, blinds and mullions) should be avoided (Verderber, 1982).

The location of these windows is also important. Because we are con-cerned with maximizing the amount of information available from the view, we should emphasize windows that face public places, that are lo-cated in front regions of the home, and that generally provide an interest-ing, changing view of the environment and other people. We may even wish to create a special indoor (for example, window seat or collection of benches) or outdoor (for example, screened porch) viewing place there. For those clients who are interested in astronomy, combining a telescope with an appropriately located window (for example, a skylight) allows them to collect information about distant stars and planets.

When we are at home, much of the information that we collect about the world comes via electronic media (for example, telephone, television, and radio). Now if we also consider some of the more recent advances in the telecommunications industry (for example, cable television and video tapes and discs), it is possible for us to learn quite a bit about our environ-ment without traveling to distant locations.

Therefore, we should make a special effort to incorporate these de-vices into the overall design of the home. Perhaps we may even create a special media room for household members to visit when they are bored. The stimulation value of a room that is deficient in either the quantity or the quality of windows and/or view amenity can be greatly enhanced in this manner (Verderber, 1982).

Learning

Exposure to complex, intense, unpredictable, and novel environments represents only one form of stimulation seeking. Alternatively, we can obtain stimulation by acquiring skills, working with our hands, searching out facts, manipulating tools and machines, and understanding technological processes.

A variety of special places can be created within the home to facilitate stimulation seeking through learning and understanding (for example, a learning center as a place for reading, studying, and learning new things).

Parents may certainly be interested in having such a place for their young children as a way of instilling positive attitudes toward learning and fostering intellectual growth. Students, who must spend many long hours in study, may also benefit from this approach. Additionally, many adults who have finished their regular schooling find that learning, as a chosen activity, is a very stimulating way to spend one's leisure time. Although many of these people take continuing education classes outside the home, the existence of a home-based learning center may provide the necessary motivation for them to pursue learning on their own.

If the client is receptive to this idea, an area can be set aside specifically for the purpose of reinforcing learning and can be furnished liberally with props that support this activity (for example, a desk, shelving for books, etc.). Furthermore, the privacy needs of people who use the area should also be considered (see Chapter 3: Social Withdrawal/Retreats for a description of a private sanctuary for study). On the other hand, for sensitive and cooperative families, the family room may be used as a learning center in which each member may pursue his/her own educational activities—as long as these behaviors are not incompatible with each other.

Alternatively, a hobby-craft area may be more appropriate for the interests of other clients. You may wish to refer back to Chapter 2 where we provided some design ideas for a variety of activity areas for both children and adults. In that chapter, we are concerned with helping people achieve environmental control by giving them things to manipulate. But the opportunity to work with one's hands satisfies the need for stimulation as well.

Computers are a rather new and innovative source of learning, excitement, and stimulation:

> *I have a loft . . . and enjoy working there on various plans and business projects. I have a feeling of comfort and privacy but also the excitement of creating business and legal projects. I like elec-*

tronic equipment and feel excited about the possibilities of using
computers to organize my business life.

Therefore, a home computer center may be designed for clients like the preceding subject. In that case, the center should probably be located in an isolated part of the home to prevent intrusion, interference, and distraction, and can be softened (for example, with living things, plants, a garden, etc.) so that the equipment does not become too much of a mechanical eyesore.

Alternatively, computers can also be used for more leisurely activities (for example, game playing) and for educational purposes, so that it might make more sense to have terminals located in various rooms. Then, the computer will be accessible to all members of the household.

In fact, computer-equipped homes are being designed in California (Dobbin, 1983). One such model contains a satellite office, which houses the main computer and functions as an electronic work station. There are also provisions for terminals to be placed in both private (for instance, master bedroom and children's suite) and public (for instance, the great room) areas of the home in order to create a variety of education and/or entertainment centers.

The computerized home, which may be the wave of the future, provides quite a challenge to the interior designer. We will have to determine how to integrate the computer into the overall design of the home and make it acceptable to all household members. And we will have to learn how to deal with the attendant problems of privacy, aesthetics, identity, etc. Hopefully, this book will sensitize the design community to these human issues, and provide some tentative solutions.

Creative Thought

Environmental stimulation and learning, as forms of stimulation seeking, both have an external focus. The emphasis is upon the environment as a source of sensory experiences or as a stimulus for learning. Under the right conditions, people are also capable of generating their own stimulation, through imagination, introspection, contemplation, and creative thinking. Now if we knew what those environmental conditions were, we could design places that facilitate this process of producing stimulation internally. Unfortunately, there appears to be little relevant psychological literature to help us; however, we will do our best to, at least, suggest some relevant environmental attributes that may satisfy the needs of clients who, in the interview, ask for "an atmosphere that is inspirational and gives freedom to creativity."

Privacy/territoriality

It would be helpful for people to have a place over which they exercise control, so that they can spend long sequences of time there concentrating on their thoughts. As one member of our sample said, "I would like a personal and private space where I could scheme and daydream." In fact, Edney and Buda (1976) found that privacy itself stimulates creativity. The suggestions presented in Chapter 3 for controlling information about the self, preventing interference from others, and facilitating social withdrawal could, therefore, be applied to the design of creative space.

Spaciousness

First of all, there is some evidence of an association between large movements, such as in dance, and creative thought. Therefore, a creative place should have sufficient floor space and floor coverings that are appropriate for free-flowing, creative exercise. The space may also be used for yoga, meditation, and other forms of relaxation—techniques that may release inhibitions and increase the production of novelty.

Second, spacious places give us a feeling of openness that may free thought of inhibitions and restrictions. In order to produce this feeling, we can design rooms with open space or use techniques to make rooms appear larger than they really are. Chapter 9 summarizes some of these methods (see Freedom/Spaciousness).

A viewing garden

What we have in mind here is to emulate the Japanese garden as a contemplative environment. As Eliovson (1978) points out, the primary goal of these gardens is to create a tranquil view from an adjoining room so that people can look outside, relax, and get lost in thought. An aesthetically pleasing composition of natural elements may border our creativity room,

if an outdoor view is available, or may be incorporated into the room itself
as an indoor garden.

Inspirational displays

Viewing art work may stimulate thought as the following subject's interview suggests:

> On the wall . . . hangs a large painting of a seaman looking out
> over the water to a ship as a gull passes overhead. I love the paint-
> ing because it has great emotional impact for me, and it is also a
> source of contemplation as I wonder what the seaman is thinking.

It's not just art itself that has the ability to stimulate the imagination;
the specific meaning of the object to the person is also very important. The
painting of the seaman was able to activate thoughts, feelings, images,
memories, and other mental processes because it represented a strong interest for our previous subject (for instance, "the nautical theme which I so
dearly love"). This line of reasoning suggests that we can help people call
up many interesting internal thoughts and sensations by personalizing a
room with art work, collected objects, and other attractive displays that are
of personal significance. Some of the ideas presented in Chapter 4 may be
applied for this purpose (see Self Definition/Personalization).

We could also create displays to stimulate the more goal-oriented
creative processes involved in people's work, in addition to the casual fan-
tasizing that we have been speaking about (for example, the awards and
achievements of a scientist, an inventor, a teacher, a writer, an artist, or a
craftsman).

Optimal level of environmental stimulation

As a general rule, when designing places to stimulate the imagination,
the amount of external stimulation should be moderate—not too much and
not too little. In an overstimulating environment, we would be too easily
distracted, too highly aroused to think in a playful and flexible manner, and
too dependent on the environment for stimulation to generate our own.
Monotonous environments also lower our ability to think in a novel way
(Maddi et al., 1962).

We have already made some suggestions in this section with respect to the type of environmental stimulation that may enhance creative imagination (for instance, gardens and displays). It may even be appropriate to use concepts from the environmental stimulation section of this chapter, particularly when dealing with clients who have high stimulation needs. Some evidence suggests that these individuals perform mental tasks more efficiently (for instance, puzzle-solving) under stimulating, even high-complexity, environmental conditions than under nonstimulating conditions.

Stimulation Reducing

When our current level of arousal is above our preferred level, we feel agitated and tense. At such a time, we are motivated to avoid highly arousing places and, instead, tend to seek out environments that have a low stimulation value. As we mentioned at the beginning of this chapter, all people feel this way at one time or another and, therefore, need some place in the home that is designed with reduced levels of stimulation. Some people may have a particularly strong need to reduce stimulation so that the entire home should be designed with this need in mind. Again, the client interview can be used as a guide in identifying these individuals; the stimulation-reducer will typically mention the characteristics and feelings associated with the low arousal homes that are discussed below.

Minimal External Stimulation

Generally speaking, when a low need for stimulation exists, space should be designed with the following characteristics, which are essentially opposite to those listed in the earlier section on environmental stimulation:

1. Simplicity: simple decor, few embellishing items, spacious rooms, uncluttered lines, closely related colors and textures, and homogeneous lighting.

2. Low intensity: cool colors, muted shades, low illumination levels, soft lighting, soft edges in furnishings, and low levels of sensory stimulation.

3. Predictability: static objects, unifying themes, matching-design elements, symmetrical arrangements, and open-plan designs.

4. Familiarity: conventional designs and styles, standard products, antiques, and heirlooms.

Relaxation

Homes that are designed according to the preceding guidelines will certainly be low in stimulation value. But when people are at home, they may require more than just minimal external stimulation; they want to release tension and relax. As Russell and Pratt (1980) point out, relaxation is not simply the opposite of excitement. Instead, relaxation is a special type of low arousal state, involving small amounts of stimulation plus pleasure. The concepts to follow, taken in conjunction with the four characteristics in the previous section, can be used in designing a relaxing environment, rather than one that may be boring and monotonous.

Nature

According to Kaplan and Kaplan (1978), there are certain stimuli that have the ability to capture our attention naturally. These stimuli seem to be associated with the wilderness environment in which we evolved as a species. Thus, we pay attention to greenery, water, fire, etc. without any effort. And, in fact, attending to these natural stimuli gives us a rest from the effortful attention that many of our daily tasks require (R. Kaplan, 1973). Similarly, Ulrich (1981) has found that viewing slides of water and vegetation reduces anxiety and helps us maintain a state of wakeful relaxation.

These studies provide a very convincing argument for incorporating natural stimuli into the design of the home. Here are some suggestions.

Candlelight and firelight can be used effectively to simulate our evolutionary environment. Water views seem to be particularly restful: "I like to sit in a chair surrounded by windows and look out over the water; it's peaceful."

Indoor/outdoor fountains could be substituted to achieve a similar effect in homes that are not adjacent to natural bodies of water. An idea for an indoor fountain has been previously mentioned in another context (see Chapter 3: Interference With Activities/Noise).

But viewing nature is not the only thing that relaxes us. Engaging in the act of gardening itself relieves tension, whereas flower growing seems to have a very strong fascination-value for us (R. Kaplan, 1973). Therefore, we should try to maximize opportunities for gardening both inside and outside the home.

It would also be desirable to create an indoor setting in which people can achieve a harmonious relationship with nature. A good example of what we mean is provided by the following interview, which shows how gentle, natural stimuli can create an easy transition between states of sleep and wakefulness:

> *I slept on a screened-in porch, surrounded by trees, in the summer months. It was cool and breezy at night, and I fell asleep to the sound of crickets. In the morning, the sun would wake me up gently.*

If this type of effect cannot be created naturally, a sunrise could be simulated with lighting, sound tapes could be used—and these effects could be preprogrammed to occur at appropriate times.

Gentle motion

When our subjects volunteered information about what is relaxing to them, they often mentioned some form of soft, gentle, repetitive movement. Some talked of a favorite rocker, swing, or glider: "I like to relax on the porch while lying on a swing." Another person described the following innovative procedure:

> *I stretch out on a water mattress or float, which fits into a kid's wading pool that is six feet in diameter. It feels just like being in a big pool on a float. I just lie there and read, or doze off in the sun, lulled by the movement of the water.*

Perhaps this idea could be adapted to an indoor space (for example, a circular pool or bath, a float, music, etc.).

Comfort

Our subjects typically associated relaxation with soft, comfortable furniture, anything that you can sink into (for example, plushy pillows, comforters, an overstuffed armchair, or a soft, comfortable couch). Some women seemed to get a feeling of peace, contentment, and comfort from pampering themselves in the bath. Much new equipment is now available for this purpose (for example, hot tubs, saunas, whirlpool baths, and enclosures that simulate various climatic conditions). An aesthetically pleasing grooming area could also be designed in the bathroom, well-outfitted and fancifully arranged with surface space, seating, mirrors, cabinets, etc. The space could be decoratively bounded so that a woman feels that she has arrived at a special place where she can spend a slowly paced relaxing time getting ready for her daily activities in the morning or preparing for bed in the evening.

Additional ideas for designing both bathrooms and bedrooms for relaxation and comfort can be found in Chapter 3: Social Withdrawal/Retreats. The concepts discussed in Chapter 5, which give the home a cozy, comfortable, and homey quality, can also be applied here (see section on Nurturance).

Privacy

Many people try to achieve privacy in order to relax. Therefore, the following design concepts discussed in Chapter 3 can be used to satisfy both needs simultaneously:

1. Control of information about the self: partitioning to help us be offstage.

2. Interference with activities: techniques for minimizing social stimulation (for example, visual distractions and noise).

3. Social withdrawal: methods for achieving physical and psychological escape (for example, retreats, places for emotional release, surrogate views, and total environments).

Congruence Between Tasks, Exteriors, and Interiors

Throughout this chapter we have argued that interiors should be designed to fit in with the client's current preferred level of arousal. But in order to completely understand the client's current need for stimulation, we must take into account what the person is doing and what area the person is living in.

First, let's talk about the nature of a person's activities. As Mehrabian (1976) points out, we need a stimulating environment in order to perform routine, repetitive tasks, or else our overall level of arousal would be too low and we would feel bored and distracted. This point is illustrated by the following personal accounts. In the first case, the stimulation value of the environment is too low; whereas, in the second example, the environment compensates quite well for the lack of arousal inherent in the routine act of dressing.

> *During the week I eat meals in my den. I sometimes get bored while I'm eating and there's nothing on TV.*

> *I get dressed in an area next to my bed. This area is good for that purpose because I can look out my window for an interesting view and listen to music on my radio.*

We would like designers to think about some of the relatively uninteresting tasks that are routinely performed in the home and the spaces in which these activities take place (for example, food preparation in the kitchen and cleaning, ironing, etc. in the laundry room). Then, suggestions from the environmental stimulation section of this chapter may be applied to make the places more attractive, colorful, imaginative, and complex. A laundry/cleaning room might include media connections, well-designed pails, attractive fabric bags for holding small items like rags, a wall-hung storage center in a bright color for storing cleaning materials, and items used in unusual and imaginative ways such as a shoe bag for hanging equipment—anything to take the dreadful monotony and oppression out of cleaning. Similarly, Mehrabian recommends a multi-purpose area for performing mechanical tasks like bill paying, in which stimulation is provided by the presence of other family members, interesting color schemes and furniture groupings, and views of nature.

On the other hand, when we are involved in interesting activities (for example, hobbies) or complex tasks that require concentration (for example, studying), it is important to minimize external stimulation. If the environment is too stimulating, a state of excessive arousal results, which not only doesn't feel good but also can interfere with our performance. Therefore, the concepts from the stimulation-reducing section of this chapter may be applied to the design of areas in which highly arousing activities occur. Along these lines, Mehrabian suggests that the social core of a home should be designed with alcoves that could be closed off from the rest of the area by sliding panels. In this manner, a more isolated and less arousing environment is provided for some highly loaded activities.

In addition to task requirements, the arousal value of the exterior environment can create differential needs for interior stimulation. Therefore, people who live in highly arousing urban environments may prefer a sleek, ultramodern, minimalist interior style, whereas people who live in rural areas may try to compensate for the lower levels of outdoor stimulation by preferring complex, ornate country-style interior designs (Mehrabian and Russell, 1974b). Mandel, Baron, and Fisher (1980) reached a similar conclusion in their study of college-campus dorms, which provided different types of window views. They found that women residents on lower floors had more posters and wall hangings than those living on upper floors. Because the authors also found that lower-floor residents perceived the view as less beautiful and less exciting than upper-floor residents, it was reasonable to assume that the women on lower floors were attempting to compensate for the lack of an interesting view by increasing the complexity of the interior decor of their rooms. This result should remind you of an earlier recommendation we made to increase the stimulation value of rooms deficient in windows, and/or view, by using media connections there.

In general, designers should try to achieve a balance between the amount of indoor stimulation on the one hand and surrounding exterior environment on the other.

AESTHETICS

— 8 —

Although psychology has traditionally emphasized the study of overt behavior, we agree with environmental psychologists (for example, Leff, 1978) who argue that the experiential nature of the human being should not be ignored. We think; we feel; we imagine; we dream—and these processes are important defining characteristics of what is human. In fact, one of the goals of a psychology of design should be to increase the quality of human experience. Designers can certainly contribute toward this noble goal by helping people to create and to appreciate beauty in the interior residential environment.

We run into problems, however, when aesthetics is used as the sole criterion for the success of a design (for instance, when other human needs are ignored). This state of affairs certainly need not exist as the design concepts presented in this book are compatible with aesthetic principles. Design can be a work of art that functions well.

In fact, the quality of the aesthetic environment, because of its association with the approach-avoidance dimension of human behavior, can set the stage for the satisfaction of other needs. In other words, people tend to remain longer (Mintz, 1956), evaluate people more positively (Maslow and Mintz, 1956), and are more willing to interact with others (Mehrabian and Russell, 1975) in pleasant, attractive settings than in unattractive ones.

However, the aesthetic environment may not function properly unless individual client definitions of beauty are taken into account by designers. Becker and Coniglio's (1975) residential survey revealed that "aesthetic was defined by each individual and not by anything approaching a norm" (p. 62). Furthermore, many residents seemed to have difficulty in identifying with "what was considered 'aesthetic' . . . in design terms" and felt that "a designer's aesthetic has little meaning for them—after all, they knew what they liked!" (p. 62). These reactions are understandable if one considers aesthetics as a mechanism of expressing individuality—a conclusion reached by Becker and Coniglio.

These reactions also form the basis for our treatment of aesthetics in this chapter. We will not attempt to review the aesthetic principles that are so familiar to the interior designer. Instead, we will identify some of the dimensions that are responsible for individual differences in aesthetic judgments and make recommendations for bringing designer- and client-definitions of beauty into agreement with each other.

Sensory Experience

Some aestheticians (for example, Osborne, 1970) view beauty as the appreciation of pure sensory experiences. Forms, colors, textures, etc. are appreciated for their own sake rather than for what they represent. Jackson (1967), in fact, sees this tendency to focus on the sensory aspects of the environment as an important dimension of personality. Thus, a sentient person is one who "notices smells, sounds, sights, tastes, and the way things feel; remembers these sensations and believes that they are an important part of life" (p. 7).

Some clients may express such a theme in the interview. For example, one member of our sample seemed to capture the very essence of the personality trait of sentience by saying the following: "Ever since I was a very young child I have been very aware of my surroundings and the moods it engendered." Furthermore, a variety of sensory experiences were revealed in the home descriptions of this individual as follows:

1. *Visual: A skylight over my bed would be nice for light and viewing the stars. . . . I would like . . . beautiful light for painting and other artistic endeavors. . . . I would like color to come from natural sources as well as what I would provide by living there (clothes, books, paints).*

2. *Auditory: I listened to the pigeons cooing in their roosts on the roof. . . . I had a . . . dressing table which held a music box.*

3. *Olfactory: I recall the smell of making wine.*

4. *Tactual: I had a . . . shade which rested on a glass bumpy base which I loved to touch. . . . I had a . . . bedroom set with drawers very deep and heavy. It had pulls . . . which my hand fit into but was hard to open. . . . I would jump onto my . . . chenille spread and feel its warmth. . . . Contrasts of texture in natural wood, stone, etc. would please my senses.*

The aesthetic design solution for clients like the previous one seems obvious; namely, an interior environment rich in sensory stimuli should be provided. In other words, designers can create facilitative environments for their clients—places that allow people to express their natural tendencies (in this case the experience of sensory aesthetics) to the fullest degree.

However, some designers may wish to go further than that. It can be argued that all people, whether or not a sensory sensitivity is expressed in the interview, should have an opportunity to engage in this very satisfying mode of experience. Leff (1978) has successfully used a number of "aesthetically-oriented cognitive sets" to facilitate the appreciation of sensory aspects of the environment. Designers, in the context of making aesthetic decisions, may wish to give some of these instructions to their clients. For example, clients can be asked to concentrate on seeing the variety of colors in the home without labeling them or to focus on "the immediate visual experience of . . . shapes, lines, textures, patterns of light and shade, repetition of similar forms" (Leff, 1978, p. 144), rather than seeing the environment as a collection of meaningful objects.

Exercises like these can sharpen the aesthetic sense and create choices that were not available before. More specifically, if clients find the sensory mode of experience to be enjoyable, they may become interested in a sensory approach to the aesthetic design of the home. In this way, designers can not only create beautiful interiors but can also increase the client's appreciation of them.

Meaning

Aesthetic judgments are also influenced by what the environment represents to us. In other words, the emotional associations that are called-up by certain design elements and arrangements can be a rich source of aesthetic pleasure. Forms, shapes, styles, materials, lighting, color, and spatial configurations (cf. Lang, 1982) all have symbolic meaning. These meanings, based upon one's own past experience, may be unique to the individual, or may represent the shared associations of a cultural group. In either case, aspects of the designed environment come to have value and beauty for us—or may even be negatively evaluated—because of what they signify.

Some examples may help to make this point clear. Bounded space may symbolize protection, closeness, and intimacy to some people but may be associated with restriction, confinement, and formality to others. Open space may be either anxiety-provoking or liberating. Red may be seen as vibrant and exciting, or overwhelming. Germans may react negatively to lightweight furniture because it is perceived as flimsy and as potentially disruptive of the order of things (Hall, 1966), whereas Americans may value it because of its flexibility.

Thus, we must find some way of dealing with both individual and group differences in aesthetic meanings or risk the potential rejection of our designs due to a lack of a fit between designer and client interpretations of the environment. Several approaches to this problem are possible: (1) We can attempt to understand and build upon existing client meanings; (2) we can create new meanings by educating the client about design; or (3) we can rely on content that may approach universal appeal.

With respect to the first alternative, the client interview is often a good source of information about personally meaningful and valued design elements. During the process of discussing and selecting design alternatives, the client's individual associations to fabrics, colors, furniture styles, etc. can be explored further. We should not only encourage this free expression of thoughts, feelings, and preferences, but we should also attempt to validate our clients' reactions. People who hire interior designers, as compared to those who do their own "decorating," may be less reluctant to express their feelings, may lack confidence in their preferential judgments—and, thus, may wish the designer to make choices for them. Although it may be easier for us to comply with these requests in the short run, it may be better in the long run to bolster the confidence of our clients. Thus, we should help them see that their aesthetic choices are valid and correct (for them) and can be integrated into a successful design concept that also conforms to the aesthetic principles of the designer.

Arnheim (1954), an expert in the psychology of art, has argued that one can derive aesthetic pleasure from viewing a work of art by understanding and appreciating how artists use their craft to express ideas and feelings. This analysis leads us to our second approach. In addition to being sensitive to individual variations in the meaning of the designed environment, designers can help their clients learn more about design and art. As clients gain insight into the manner in which form, color, scale, etc. are used to create beautiful interiors, the process of design acquires new meaning for them; and, as a result, their aesthetic appreciation of design is enhanced.

There is some experimental evidence that people consistently prefer pictures of natural settings to those of built environments (for example, Kaplan, Kaplan, and Wendt, 1972). These data have led some psychologists to conclude that natural content per se is an important environmental-preference variable. We have also been impressed by the number of references made in our interviews to nature as an aesthetically pleasing interior design element. Although there may be danger in relying upon universal principles of beauty given that individual differences in aesthetic response are expected, the meaning and significance of the natural/artificial distinction for people in general appears to be well documented. Therefore, we would like to present the following partial list of techniques for creating interiors high in naturalness:

1. Natural light: A large proportion of our subjects asked for rooms (for example, "favorite room—sunshiny family room") and areas (for example, "a table . . . in front of a sunny bay window") filled with "sun, sun, sun." Natural light should, therefore, be used whenever possible. Simulations and substitutions can be employed in rooms that get little sun (for example, lamps that are strong in the yellow-red range or a sunrise effect created with appropriate lighting technology).

2. Sky effect: It was quite common for our subjects to express a desire for skylights in various home locations: the bedroom ("a skylight over my bed would be nice for . . . viewing the stars"); the kitchen ("under the skylight I'd like a sitting area, wicker couch and seats, coffee table, etc."); and the foyer ("after the ascent to the top floor, a sky-lighted foyer greeted me and I got a lift"). Sky effects can also be simulated (for example, with starlike and/or cloudlike images on ceilings), or a total landscape effect can be created (for example, with blue overhead, green underfoot, and natural simulations such as trees and flowers on vertical surfaces).

3. Natural materials: Perhaps the oft-mentioned preference for wood on walls ("I'd like all wood walls in my kitchen of the future"); floors ("I had a dark wood floor with small throw rugs"); and furnishings ("I would like light wood furniture—teak or oak") is due to its perception as a natural substance.

4. Natural colors: Although the perception of color itself is pleasurable, the source of color can affect its value as an aesthetic stimulus. Thus, the experience of color can be enhanced by using colors that come from natural sources (for example, flowers, plants, and natural materials) that represent the local geography, or that symbolize favorite—but more distant— places.

5. Water and vegetation: We have discussed ideas for incorporating gardens, plant areas, fountains, etc. into the interior decor of the home in other chapters (for instance, Chapter 2: Control of Space/Partitions; Chapter 3: Interference with Activities/Noise). Our subjects frequently requested such things as "a big bathroom with a greenhouse" or "a secret small adjoining walled garden with rocks and running water," so that an intimate relationship is achieved with nature inside the home. Alternatively, a purely visual relationship with nature is also a high priority item as views of greenery (for example, "a lovely garden surrounding the house so that when I looked out the window I would see flowers and trees") and water ("I have always enjoyed outdoor views, particularly water—lake or ocean") were highly preferred.

6. Nonvisual experiences: In addition to visual sensations, people appreciate the sounds of nature (for example, birds, running water—experienced naturally or through sound tapes), the natural fragrances of flowers and plants, and the characteristic textures of particular plant materials. Many public nature areas contain "gardens of the senses" specially designed to appeal to a variety of the senses. Plantings selected for touch (for example, lamb's ear and leather-leaf viburnum); scent (for example, lemon balm and bayberry); and taste (for example, various vegetables and herbs) could also provide similar experiences in indoor/outdoor private residential gardens.

7. Seasonal change: We derive pleasure from viewing nature partially because of the welcome change in seasons that is clearly represented there. One subject reported such an experience as follows:

> My room . . . looked out onto a typical Italian garden with staked
> tomatoes, symmetrically planted, and headed with two fig trees.
> The changing of seasons was paramount to me.

Perhaps color, lighting, texture, and furnishings could be employed in the interior environment to simulate seasonal change, particularly for those people who live in areas with homogeneous climates and, therefore, are deprived of this experience. For example, the kitchen might represent spring (for example, wicker furniture, lots of green plants and green, white, and yellow colors); the bath might be summer (for example, lush plants, flowers, rich colors, water, and steam)—and the general concept of associating rooms with particular seasons could be continued throughout the home.

Stimulus Properties

Much of the experimental research on aesthetics has been concerned with establishing a relationship between particular attributes of the environment (for example, complexity) and affective responses. Although there have been some exceptions, research has generally supported the view that people prefer intermediate degrees of complexity. According to Berlyne (1974), a certain amount of complexity is desirable in order to maintain an optimal level of arousal (see Chapter 7), but high levels of complexity induce too much uncertainty and, therefore, may be aversive.

This analysis suggests to us that aesthetic judgment may be a result of the interaction between two needs: variety and order. A number of researchers and theorists in the areas of aesthetics and environmental preference appear to take such an approach in their writing. S. Kaplan (1975) maintains that we are influenced by two oppositional tendencies: the need to acquire new information about the environment and the need to make sense of things. According to Platt (1961), aesthetic enjoyment involves the perception of "a pattern that contains the unexpected" (p. 403). Similarly, Findlay and Field (1982) argue that "the interaction of complexity and continuity . . . forms the basis of an aesthetic experience" (p. 152).

According to this view of aesthetics, designers should strive for a balance between the stimulation value of an interior environment and the degree to which that environment is perceived as orderly and organized. Techniques from Chapter 7: Stimulation Seeking/Environmental Stimulation and Chapter 6: Perceptual Organization may be appropriately combined for that purpose. For example, cohesive variety can be achieved with coordinating, rather than matching, colors; combinations of diversity and repetition in pattern, shape, and form; and dissimilar furnishings balanced horizontally and/or vertically, or tied together through underlying similarities in style, texture, and color.

Of course, designers regularly use methods such as these to create aesthetically pleasing designs. We merely wish to point out why these techniques work so well. However, there is one complicating factor. Although aesthetic appreciation may be the result of some optimal combination of variety and order, what is optimal varies from individual to individual.

According to Wohlwill (1974), people get used to particular levels of diversity and patterning in the environment as a function of their prior experience with these levels. In this way, a relatively stable adaptation level is formed, which acts as a frame of reference for making judgments (including aesthetic ones) about current and future environments. If the perceived amount of environmental stimulation is similar to, or deviates slightly from, adaptation level, a person is likely to respond favorably; however, large deviations from adaptation level are experienced as stressful.

Thus, adaptation level theory suggests that designers may have to decide on how much variety and orderliness to include in their designs for individual clients, so that the quantity of these attributes does not deviate drastically from the client's adaptation level. Certainly, the interview is a valuable source of information in this regard. Adaptation levels, which are influenced by past and present environmental experiences, can be roughly estimated by the relative salience of variety- and order-themes in home descriptions; and interiors can be designed accordingly. To simplify this determination, we suggest that three relationships between these need-themes be identified: an emphasis upon variety, an emphasis upon order, and an equal emphasis upon both. The following interviews and their analyses serve as examples of these respective relationships:

> *The bright yellow flowered wallpaper dazzled me. . . . I had a window from which I could observe a marvelously complex arrangement of trees and bushes surrounded by flowers. . . . The dining room was one of the most active rooms in the house . . . playing cards or watching old movies used to keep us busy so often. . . . The dining room now has a gorgeous built-in hutch filled with vases, statues, and knickknacks which seem to create a visual pleasure filled with diversity. . . . I always took pride in the fact that . . . every room was kept neat and straightened.*

Analysis: The frequent mention of environmental attributes such as complexity, activity, and diversity suggests that this person has adapted to, and prefers, a high degree of variety. However, the last statement implies that order is also important to this individual—albeit in a secondary manner.

I dislike . . . clutter and the unorganized sense of things. . . . It bothers me if nothing's in order and things don't seem to coordinate. . . . But I don't like bare empty things—total neatness and order.

Analysis: Order seems to predominate in this interview, but not to the total exclusion of some degree of variety as the last statement suggests.

My room is very noncontrived . . . but is put together with a total color scheme which balances it out to create continuity. . . . I picture myself in a room which has big, flowing space and nonsequential patterns all over, although it would be tied together with color to provide some sense of order.

Analysis: Unlike the first two subjects, who seem to stress one need over the other, this person appears to have adapted to an environment with equal amounts of novelty, variety, continuity, and order.

Distance versus Engagement

Berleant (1982) distinguishes between two philosophical approaches to aesthetic perception: an aesthetic of distance and an aesthetic of engagement. According to the former view, the perceiver and the aesthetic object are conceptualized as separate entities in both a physical and a psychological sense. The environment is meant to inspire awe in the viewer as a purely visual experience and to be contemplated and appreciated for its monumentality and symmetry. On the other hand, the latter approach emphasizes the inseparability of the perceiver and the perceived—a fusion of participant and place. The person is invited to experience the environment in all its dimensions rather than remain at a distance from it.

Although Berleant is primarily concerned with the implications of this distinction for the aesthetic design of exterior environments (for example, city planning, highway engineering, and wilderness management), we think that his analysis is also relevant to interior residential design, as we were able to identify the same two aesthetic themes—distance and engagement—in a number of our interviews.

The following subjects seem to be expressing a desire for aesthetic distance—an appreciation for the visual contemplation of interior architectural features, art objects, and the panoramic landscape:

I remember feeling awe at the high ceilings and delicately carved moldings.

I like to admire the interior structure of the house.

I would feel elated in a room with large windows. . . . One window would give me a panoramic view of the city, the other would overlook a sculpture garden.

An aesthetic approach that includes visually exciting and awe-inspiring design elements such as the following would be appropriate for these individuals: shimmering fabrics, museumlike displays (for example, fine pedestals for sculpture), collections of expensive objects, palatial entrances, high ceilings or the visual impression of height, dramatic outdoor views (framed with an arch or with lighting), architectural details, tapestries, stained glass, lead crystal chandeliers, and spectacular lighting effects.

In contrast, the following subjects appear to prefer aesthetic engagement—a home environment that is attractive but is also welcoming to the individual.

I would like a stylish, nice place to be able to enjoy and feel comfortable in.

The living room was nice, but not nearly as homey and comfortable as I would have liked.

I would like an area of welcoming, enticing comfort, a place that makes you feel good.

In these cases, designers may wish to rely upon the following concepts: total sensory involvement (see Chapter 4: Distinctiveness/Vivid Sensory Experiences, Participation/Hands-On Experiences and Chapter 7: Intensity/Sensory Involvement), personalization of space (see Chapter 4: Self-Definition/Personalization), comfort/warmth (see Chapter 5: Nurturance), and bonding with the local environment (for example, local materials and regional designs—also see Chapter 4: Distinctiveness/Dwelling Identity).

CHOICE

— 9 —

We react negatively when our thoughts, feelings, and actions are restricted. Instead, we like to have behavioral options and feelings of freedom. In short, maintaining freedom of choice is an important human motive (Brehm, 1966).

Furthermore, the design of a physical setting is one factor that affects the extent to which freedom of choice is achieved (Proshansky, Ittelson, and Rivlin, 1970). Places themselves can be perceived as either limiting/constraining or free and open—an observation strongly supported by Tognoli and Horwitz's (1982) residential interviews as well as our own. The goal of the design concepts presented in this chapter, therefore, is to expand human possibilities by creating interiors that maximize freedom of choice.

Behavioral Diversity

In one sense choice means having options and alternatives so that we can engage in a variety of behaviors of our own choosing in the home. Behavioral freedom is particularly important to house-bound individuals (for example, the elderly and the disabled). These people require a home environment that increases the range of behavior open to them. Peterson, Wekerle, and Morley (1978) argue that women are similarly dependent upon the home as a mechanism for maximizing behavioral opportunities because, even in the face of changing sex roles, women still spend much time there and have a significant amount of responsibility for household management.

With respect to others, the need for choice may develop over time as a function of prior interactions with the environment. Proshansky (1978) makes such a point with respect to urban dwellers. A complex urban environment contains a variety of functionally distinct settings including parks, museums, theaters, stores, office buildings, apartments, streets, etc. Additionally, within each type of setting there is considerable variation (for example, different house forms and various modes of transportation). In the process of using these diverse facilities, the urban resident learns not only how to make choices but also to expect them. In this manner, a need for environments that supply sufficient and appropriate choices is created. As Proshansky puts it, freedom of choice becomes a significant part of the urbanite's self-identity.

We think that this same sequence of events may take place in transactions with interior environments. In other words, we may become adapted to a home environment that has provided a variety of choices in the past and come to desire such a place in the future. Collecting interview data with respect to past, present, and future residences has allowed us to observe this developmental process unfold. For example, one of our subjects lived in a highly differentiated room as a child, which provided for a number of optional activities:

> *My room was large enough for a sitting area, a study area, and a place for sleeping. It also had a window seat, which I used for reading and thinking.*

As a function of these early experiences, it appears that a demand for freedom of choice was established with respect to a home for the future: "In the future, I would like a sitting area in my room for eating breakfast and reading the paper, a separate area for dressing, and an area for working and studying."

The design concepts to follow are to be used for those individuals who, by nature of current circumstance or prior history, demonstrate the need to choose between diverse environmental experiences. Although desired activities may vary from individual to individual, thus altering specific design requirements, the ability to choose among these activities is of paramount importance to all—and is therefore the primary focus of this chapter.

Territoriality

According to Proshansky, Ittelson, and Rivlin (1970), "one way to achieve . . . freedom of choice is through the ability to control what goes on in defined areas of space . . ." (p. 178). When occupying a clearly defined territory, the territory holder has the right of "choice in behavior type" (Edney, 1976, p. 39). This right lowers inhibitions for engaging in desired activities and makes it legitimate for the owner to modify the territory so that it suits a variety of behaviors. In contrast, there are restrictions placed upon the behavior of a visitor in another person's territory (Edney, 1976). Although these restrictions are not as severe as for nonresidents, members of the same household will typically respect each other's territorial rights and voluntarily take on the behavioral role of "visitor" when they enter personally controlled areas such as bedrooms, dens, and home offices.

The preceding arguments further document the case for providing all members of the household with a personal territory. At first glance, it may appear that the more enclosed a space is (for example, a separate room, one of the environmental enclosures that we spoke of earlier), the more options are open to the individual. Although it is true that people are more apt to engage in private activities and personalization of the environment in enclosed spaces, these spaces may produce a condition of isolation and, therefore, decrease options for engaging in social behavior. One of our subjects discussed such an outcome as follows:

> *My work area is located in part of the front room on the first floor of a two-story house. It's too open and it's really not private enough for me. I could have located my office in a room on the second floor, but I opted for having the office downstairs so as not to be too far away from my family and my other activities in the house.*

Perhaps the ideal solution for this person would be to have a separate room on the first floor to be used as an office. (No such space was available in this case.) Alternatively, other boundary-defining techniques (see Chapter 2: Control of Space/Territoriality), which involve a combination of physical and psychological separation (for example, partitions and screens), could be employed to partially increase options for privacy while maintaining the possibility of social contact.

This example brings up an important general point about the selection of boundary control mechanisms for defining territories. Specifically, clients should be questioned concerning the uses that the territory is to be put to and the trade-offs they are willing to make. Then, a boundary technique can be selected involving the proper degree of separation and connection in order to fit the client's goals and priorities (see also Chapter 3: Control of Information about the Self and Privacy Regulation).

With respect to young children, a corner of a room in the social core of the home may provide sufficient territorial definition to increase freedom of choice as the following childhood recollection suggests: "I remember cozy corners in which I was allowed to pursue whatever activity—reading, drawing, day-dreaming—that suited my fancy." This arrangement also allows parent and child to be accessible to each other.

Furnishings for Functional Differentiation and Flexibility

The general point we would like to make in this section is that the manner in which a room is furnished affects the variety of behaviors that can occur there. Think of furnishings as "staging props"—things that can be added to a space to "create new opportunities for activity" (Zeisel, 1981, p. 103). Conceptualized in this way, furnishings provide environmental support for various activities—initiating and maintaining behavior that is congruent with the environment (for example, people will sit and read in a space with comfortable seating and good lighting, socialize in a lounge, etc.).

In order to illustrate how behavioral diversity can be increased by the introduction of props, we will briefly describe the results of T.L. Miller (1978). The setting for this study was a day room in an institution for the retarded. Miller observed that this room, practically empty except for some plastic chairs, was used primarily for isolated passive behavior (for example, sitting alone and sleeping). Furnishings were then added to differentiate the room into four functionally distinct zones: an arts and crafts area, a lounge, an area for games and music, and an empty space. Following the introduction of these design alterations, it was observed that behavior diversity increased in all areas of the room as residents began to engage in mixed active (for example, watching television and housekeeping) and social (for example, playing games and talking) behavior. Even the empty area became a locus for social behavior, indicating that an unfinished space embedded in a highly differentiated room is more functional than an empty room.

Although the previous study was performed with a special population in an institutional environment, we think that freedom of choice can be similarly increased in the home by using appropriate furnishings to create functionally differentiated spaces. Such an approach would have been useful for one of our subjects, who described the living room as "empty, underused, and possibly superfluous." This room was practically devoid of furniture just as the institutional day room was.

Alternatively, furnishings can be selected to create a condition of room flexibility. According to High and Sundstrom (1977), flexible rooms—those that contain movable, rather than fixed, furniture—maximize freedom of choice because they can be put to a variety of uses through various furniture re-arrangements. This hypothesis was confirmed by their study of college dormitory rooms. In this study, flexible rooms were used more often than nonflexible rooms for a variety of interpersonal activities (for example, studying with friends, partying, talking, and visiting).

In the home environment, room flexibility can be achieved in a variety of ways. Adjustable and multifunctional furnishings can be used, in addition to those that are simply portable (see Chapter 2: Furnishings/Soft Architecture). And underdesigned areas can be created, which accommodate optional activities through various transformations (see Chapter 2: Furnishings/Underdesigned Space). In both these cases, the ability to manipulate the environment not only increases feelings of control, but also facilitates freedom of choice.

These feelings are just as important for children as for adults. Flexible furnishings should, therefore, be preferred for children's rooms in order to avoid experiences like the following: "I hated my furniture because it . . . was all connected together so I could not re-arrange my room very much."

Designs for Primary and Secondary Purposes

Typically, we attempt to construct an environment, selecting and arranging props in such a manner so that we can accomplish our primary purpose in using that setting. The following subject, for example, described the props needed to construct a reading environment. "The best place for reading books was propped up in bed with a warm light and plenty of equipment—a radio, tables for books, writing supplies, and access to food and drink."

Designers can, therefore, increase the client's ability to choose specific desired activities by looking for descriptions like the preceding one in the interview and making recommendations with respect to the props needed to support these behaviors. This role demands that the designer understand the environmental requirements for various behaviors. Farrenkopf and Roth (1980) mention a number of such factors that seem to be important for people in general across a variety of settings. These variables, as well as others, are discussed in Chapter 6: Organization of Activities. Additional idiosyncratic requirements for the physical environment can be gleaned from client descriptions of favorite activities, supplemented with probe questions such as the following: Exactly where do you perform a particular activity? Why is this location conducive to the activity? What are the shortcomings of the chosen location? What places would not be selected and why?

In this manner, we were able to determine that the following environmental properties were important to a person who preferred to eat breakfast in the bedroom rather than the kitchen:

1. Relaxation: "It is relaxing to eat in the peace and quiet of my room, too many people talking in the kitchen, noise is screened out in the basement where my room is located."

2. Privacy: "People are least likely to disturb me in my room."

3. Control: "I have control over the noise level and the topic being discussed when I'm in my room."

4. Space: "The kitchen table is too small. Limited space [in my room] makes me feel cramped."

5. Comfort: "It's warm in the basement during the winter, while the rest of the house is markedly cooler in the summer."

6. Variety: "I enjoy looking out the window during breakfast, but I can't do this in my room. I get bored after a period of time."

7. Contact with nature: "Hard to see and feel the weather for the day."

Some of the environmental attributes mentioned in the descriptions of people's activities in the home seem to be directly related to the primary purpose of using the environment (for example, light for reading or surface space for eating). Others seem to be indirectly related (for example, "When my work is frustrating, I go to my piano, which is within reach of my desk, and more or less beat my frustrations out") or unrelated to the primary purpose (for example, access to food and drink while reading or knowledge of the weather while eating).

It is extremely important for designers to recognize this multidimensional quality of people's goals and corresponding design requirements, for "any physical setting that provides many alternatives for the satisfaction of a primary purpose and the satisfaction of related and unrelated subsidiary purposes obviously provides cc..siderable freedom of choice" (Proshansky, Ittelson, and Rivlin, 1970, p. 175). If a place is not designed for secondary purposes, people tend to use the setting in a purely functional manner—doing whatever is essential and then leaving as soon as possible, rather than engaging in the full range of behavior. In fact, such an environment does not fulfill the primary purpose very well either. The following interview illustrates these points:

> I do most of my work at my desk downstairs, where my telephone is located. I could use it as a place of enjoyment and relaxation too except that there's not enough room, it's too cluttered, it's uncomfortable to sit, and I have to worry about disturbing others or being disturbed. Now I do what has to be done there. It serves its purpose, but only for short periods of time.

Usable Space

Different activities have different spatial requirements, so that the more space you have, the more things you can do with it. The availability of space also increases the possibilities for functional differentiation and furniture re-arrangement. One of our subjects discussed the effect of spatial availability upon freedom of choice in the following manner:

> Limited space makes me feel cramped, so that I can only spend a certain amount of time in my room a day. I do not invite friends to the room because it is small. I don't think others would be comfortable in this . . . space. I only have a certain limited number of activities in this room.

Of course, we would all love to have a lot of space; it is indeed a luxury to both designer and client. Unfortunately, many people must live in the compact houses, tight spaces, and high density conditions of today's housing market, where space is at a premium. Even under these conditions, with the amount of (floor) space held constant, it is still possible to maximize choices by increasing the amount of usable space through design. Schiffenbauer et al. (1977), for example, compared rooms of identical size, which differed in the placement of the door. In one set of rooms the door opened onto a closet, but in the other set of rooms the door swept through a space which could have been used for other purposes. Thus, the second set of rooms contained less usable space than the first. Although the authors did not directly assess the effect of usable space upon behavioral diversity, they did find that the rooms with less usable space were seen as smaller.

Additional space-saving techniques and general issues involved in the use of space are discussed elsewhere (see Chapter 6: Household Maintenance/Orderly Use of Space). Furthermore, space use should be planned carefully so that incompatible activities are not located in adjacent areas (see Chapter 3: Interference with Activities/Behavioral Planning). If they are, people are likely to cope with potential interference by restricting their use of these areas as well as the range of behaviors that occur there.

Alternative Areas

In addition to giving people choices in behavior type, we can provide different places within the home for performing the same activity—as long as space permits such an arrangement. People would then be free to make locational choices depending upon current moods and preferences. A number of our subjects reported variations in the location of their activities, an outcome that suggests the importance of this form of choice. The following individuals made locational choices for reading, exercising, and being alone, respectively:

I read books in various parts of my childhood home. . . . The best place for this was propped up in bed. . . . I also liked to read on the porch . . . on a swing with outdoor light and cool breezes.

I do my exercises in the bedroom, den, or downstairs recreation room.

During the summer the best place to be was on our front porch. . . . It was the perfect place to escape both physically and mentally. . . . The upstairs seems like a separate world . . . because at times I become so carried away with what I am doing, and with the silence, that I forget where I am.

Creative Solutions

Generally speaking, an environment that satisfies a wide variety of needs provides its occupants with many choices. According to this view, the design concepts presented throughout this book perform a dual function; that is, they satisfy the need for which they were intended and, as an incidental consequence, satisfy the need for choice as well. However, the design process would be much too complex if we attempted to use techniques from all the chapters and thought of these techniques, and their associated needs, as if they were independent of each other. They are not; in fact, we have attempted to illustrate the interrelationships between needs throughout the preceding chapters.

In the introduction, we offered some suggestions for simplifying the design process. Among them was the idea of searching for "creative solutions"—using design concepts that simultaneously satisfy a number of different needs. An environment designed in this manner provides the client with choices for need-satisfaction, while reducing the complexity of the designer's task. The following list summarizes some of these techniques and their uses:

1. Territorial boundaries: Define areas of control, provide visual and/or acoustic barriers for privacy, aid in the perceptual organization of space, and increase visual complexity.

2. Soft architecture: Contributes to feelings of personal control, facilitates privacy regulation, enhances self-evaluation, and results in functionally complex interiors.

3. Enclosures: Are associated with feelings of control, can be used to achieve solitude, provide a nurturant environment, and facilitate intimate relationships.

4. Personalization of space: Contributes to feelings of ownership, helps to define the self, makes us feel secure, and is a source of visual complexity and a stimulus for interaction.

5. Sensory involvement: Facilitates attachment to and identification with the home, raises arousal level, and provides aesthetic pleasure.

6. Natural elements: Define spaces, allow us to produce effects (gardening), are associated with creativity, provide relaxing experiential states, enhance aesthetic meaning, and facilitate cooperative social relationships.

7. Windows and surrogate views: Yield privacy through psychological escape, are a source of information about the environment, help us relax, and facilitate perceptions of room friendliness.

8. Displays: Signal family permanence, help us organize our activities, and provide inspiration for creativity.

9. Association with the past: Facilitates attachment to place, contributes to self-definition and self-evaluation, affords permanence/security, and adds to the uniqueness/variety of the home environment.

10. Activity areas: Give us the experience of manipulating our environment and serve the need for variety by providing places for learning.

Freedom

Whereas behavioral diversity, our first dimension of choice, deals with what people are able to do in the home, freedom is concerned more with feelings, perceptions, and attitudes. We like to feel free, open, comfortable, uninhibited, and unconstrained. The following interviews, taken from a family we have worked with, provide an excellent illustration of this second dimension of choice—as a strong freedom theme is present throughout.

> *I like water, plants, big windows, hammocks, comfortable furniture. I like a light, airy look.*

> *I don't like the way it seems that nothing is really very comfortable feeling or looking.*

> *Perhaps a feeling of connection with nature or the outside environment is the most important thing to me. . . . I like windows with no curtains, hanging plants, stark white walls . . . and open space.*

> *I would like my present home to be light, spacious. . . . My ideal future home will be open to the outdoors with a view of water. It will be light and . . . casual.*

> *I would like . . . skylights, light modern furniture . . . a patio to sit outside with flowers and nice trees . . . some wide open spaces.*

Spaciousness

Spacious places are typically associated with feelings of freedom and openness, whereas a lack of space often engenders feelings of crowding, confinement, crampedness, and constraint. However, the actual amount of space is not the only variable that affects the perception of spaciousness and freedom. As we mentioned before, rooms with more usable space are seen as larger than less usable, but equal-sized, rooms (Schiffenbauer et al., 1977). Designers have typically employed a number of other functionally equivalent techniques to perceptually expand a space. Some of these methods, along with others suggested by research in crowding and environmental design, are summarized below because of their implications for freedom of choice.

1. Brightness: Research has demonstrated that increases in brightness, produced by color, sunlight, or auxiliary light sources, are associated with greater perceived spaciousness. Baum and Davis (1976) found that light-colored rooms were perceived as being larger, less crowded, and less stuffy than dark-colored rooms. Similarly, the more sunlight a room receives, the larger (Schiffenbauer et al., 1977) and less crowded (Mandel, Baron, and Fisher, 1980) it appears to be. Laboratory studies of various lighting arrangements have also revealed that impressions of spaciousness can be augmented by increasing the intensity of an overhead lighting system (for example, Flynn et al., 1973).

2. Uniformity: A monochromatic color scheme increases perceived room size through figure-ground fusion. Uniformly illuminated spaces also appear larger than those lit in a nonuniform manner (Flynn et al., 1973).

3. Simplicity: Simple quiet spaces (for example, with minimal furnishings, little architectural detail, and a lack of variety of shape and form) are typically seen as open, spacious ones.

4. Transparency/reflection: Surfaces done in materials such as glass, acrylic, mirror, or metal take up little visual space and/or create additional space through reflection (Crane, 1982). Visual access into other areas can be enhanced if these spaces are defined with partial, open (for example, filigree), or symbolic barriers. And according to Desor's (1972) study, partial partitions (for instance, a waist-high barrier or a glass wall) can reduce perceptions of crowding as effectively as a solid wall for those people using the partitioned spaces. Research also suggests that the expanded visual access provided by windows increases perceptions of spaciousness (Kaye and Murray, 1982) and roominess (Baron et al., 1976). Windows on upper floors seem to be particularly useful in this regard as several studies have found that the perceived size of windowed rooms is augmented as floor height increases (Mandel, Baron, and Fisher, 1980; Schiffenbauer et al., 1977)—although the exact mechanism responsible for this effect is unclear. (Suggestions for increasing the "windowness" of an environment have been presented earlier in Chapter 7: Stimulation Seeking/New Information About the World.) Additionally, designers often combine transparent surfaces with reflective ones (for example, placing a mirror opposite a window view) in order to magnify the spaciousness effect (Crane, 1982).

5. Order: Samuelson and Lindauer (1976) found that a neat room was seen as emptier and larger than a messy room. Both rooms contained the same items, the only difference being that the items were arranged in an orderly manner in the neat room. These researchers thought that the decreased visual diversity of the neat room shifted attention away from objects to walls and expanses, producing an "increased consciousness of area" and, thus, room size. This perspective is useful as it suggests that other techniques that increase awareness of spaces rather than objects would also lead to a sense of spaciousness. The results can also be interpreted in another way. A neat room provides cues that facilitate the perceptual organization of space. Organized spaces seem to contain less things, and thus, appear larger than disorganized spaces. Accordingly, the design concepts offered throughout Chapter 6 should contribute to both order and spaciousness.

6. Ceiling height: Savinar (1975) found that ceiling height tends to reduce feelings of crowding. Besides making structural modifications, designers typically use low furniture and vertical lines to enhance the perception of ceiling height. The feeling of height might also be increased by using a detailed pattern on walls along with a similar pattern on the ceiling that is either smaller in scale or contains less detail. Because distant objects are less clear and smaller than objects that are closer to us, the ceiling would appear to be farther away than it really is.

7. Room shape: Rectangular rooms appear to be larger (Sadalla and Oxley, 1984) and less crowded (Desor, 1972) than square rooms of the same size. Irregular shapes within a space (for example, cloverleaves, L-shapes, and alcoves) are perceived as separate places (Zeisel, 1981), so that the presence of these irregularities may make the space appear to be more extensive. These effects may be produced through structural alteration or approximated through appropriate furniture placement.

8. Scale: Lightweight furniture in plastics, light woods, etc. seems to take up less space than massive, heavy furniture. Objects and wall hangings (as figure) that are kept small in relation to the ground give the effect of small things in a large area.

Open-Plan Design

For my family, the kitchen has always been a combination living room-den-kitchen. . . . Ideally the kitchen should be more open to the living and dining rooms. It should be more like one large room divided into areas.

The preceding subject is expressing a desire for an open plan (that is, many activities located in one large space) rather than a closed one (that is, separate rooms for different activities). Weale, Croake, and Weale (1982) have attributed the re-emergence of the open plan in the residential environment to today's informal style of living. For our purposes, a preference for open-space design reflects a need for freedom from barriers and other restrictions: "I would like to have a feeling of openness in my environment— fewer obstructing walls."

However, in order for this design to provide freedom of choice and flexibility in shared spaces, other related needs must be addressed. In this regard, perhaps we can learn something from the extensive research that has evaluated the effectiveness of open-plan offices and schools. This research (for example, Sundstrom and Sundstrom, 1983) has identified the following problems associated with open plans: auditory (for example, conversation noise) and visual (for example, movement of other people) distraction, privacy/control of information about the self (for example, personal conversations and phone calls overheard and observation of errors and embarrassing behavior by others), privacy/interference (for example, interruptions and intrusions), control (for example, inability to regulate ambient factors and insufficient territorial definition).

Small-scale design interventions have been successful in alleviating some of these problems, such as Evans and Lovell's (1979) use of sound-absorbent partitions to define boundaries, reduce distractions, and increase privacy. Techniques presented in earlier chapters might have a similar effect in the home environment. Separate territories can be defined using methods that give people a sense of personal control and protect them from noise, visual distractions, and privacy invasions (see Chapter 2: Control of Space; Chapter 3: Control of Information about the Self and Interference with Activities). People can also be given the ability to control aspects of the ambient environment in these territories (see Chapter 2: Control of the Ambient Environment). However, it is important to be selective in the choice of these design concepts so that the feeling of openness/freedom of the open-plan design is preserved.

High Places

One of our subjects recalled a number of preferred childhood spaces, which had one characteristic in common—height:

*I had a dormer window with a ledge just wide enough to sit on.
My room was three stories above the ground on that side of the
house and was overlooking a very steep hill. I liked getting out on
that ledge . . . and looking out through the huge oak trees down to
the street far below. . . . I liked climbing a dogwood tree in the
yard, sitting at the very top and singing. . . . We had high ceilings. My closet had a sort of cupboard storage area above it. I
liked climbing into that place and lying there.*

Later in the interview, this subject expressed a desire for openness in
the home environment. We think there is a connection between this desire
and the high places of the childhood home which were previously described. Berrill (1955), for one, seems to attribute the human desire for
freedom to our evolutionary past when our arboreal ancestors lived in the
free, open environment of the treetops. Perhaps the special fascination of
the tree-house and the appeal of aerial views can be similarly explained by
evolutionary principles.

However, one need not resort to evolutionary theory to explain the relationship between height and freedom. In Chapter 2: Control of Space, we
noted that elevated places are seen as distinct areas and, therefore, can be
used to reduce negative feelings of crowding, constraint, and a lack of freedom of choice associated with small, shared spaces. On the basis of this
line of reasoning, we recommend that the experience of height be incorporated into the interior design of homes (for example, with lofts, platforms,
bunk beds, ceiling-suspended swing chairs, and visual vistas).

Contact with Nature

The openness and spaciousness of the outdoors can be brought indoors
in order to achieve a casual, informal atmosphere in which people can
throw off inhibitions and freely be themselves. (Other ideas for creating informal space are discussed in Chapter 10: Designing for Characteristic Interaction Styles.) Tognoli and Horwitz (1982) interviewed a person who
expressed such a desire for an indoor/outdoor connection "as a source of
freedom":

You could actually just wake up in the morning, get out of bed, and dive
into the ocean. . . . Everything that was happening outside would be part

of what was happening inside—meaning the water or the land would in some way become part of the environment that you would feel when you were in the house (p. 325).

Although it is rarely possible to achieve such a spectacular effect, other techniques can be used to transcend the separation of indoor and outdoor space. A variety of plant types do quite well indoors, including free-standing trees and shrubs, trailers and climbers, flowering plants, groupings of small plants, and tropical plants in terrariums (Weale, Croake, and Weale, 1982). Furthermore, if outdoor greenery can be viewed through a window, indoor plants, containers, and/or floor materials can be selected to link the interior environment with the garden (Weale, Croake, and Weale, 1982).

Windows can also be used in other ways to accomplish the same goal. For example, the window could open onto a Japanese viewing garden, providing residents with an opportunity to escape psychologically into a private world of contemplation. Any beautiful natural view would do; but the Japanese garden is designed to maximize the illusion of depth/spaciousness (cf. Eliovson, 1978)—an outcome which enhances feelings of freedom. A balcony can be integrated into the living area by eliminating obstructing window treatments and furnishing it appropriately. And, if an attractive landscape view is available, outdoor lighting can be installed on the trees and the balcony, creating a beautiful mural effect for the evening. Finally, if windows and/or natural views are absent, substitutions can be made (for example, a mural, a skylight, or an indoor garden of stone and sand).

SOCIABILITY

— 10 —

The home is an important context for the satisfaction of social needs. Family members relate to each other on a personal basis: "I would like my home to be a comfortable, loving place for us and for our children to grow up in." Closeness and friendship are shared with others: "My present dwelling is a place where friends and relatives are always welcome, a place that reflects warmth, love, and friendliness." And people entertain guests in a variety of ways (for example, "small groups . . . for dinner and an evening of stimulating conversation" or "parties with lots of people and loud music").

The designer can play a significant role here by creating settings that are—in the words of one of our subjects—"conducive to conviviality." Of course, it would be incorrect to view design as a cause or a determinant of behavior; relationships, or at least the potential for their formation, must be there already. However, the use of certain design elements and techniques can provide environmental support for these relationships and, perhaps, make them more satisfying.

Family Cohesiveness

Many of our subjects told warm, touching stories of the family getting together, as a whole or in smaller units, to share a meal, an activity, or an intimate moment. Feelings of satisfaction and togetherness were also expressed when family members were doing separate things, but were in the

145

same general locale. The design concepts to follow are, therefore, offered to facilitate the experience of family cohesiveness.

Family Gathering Areas

Obviously, if family members are to interact, they must be proximal to each other. Therefore, we must provide centrally located spaces that are accessible to all family members (Mehrabian, 1976)—places that are used naturally and have something to offer for everyone.

In many homes the kitchen fulfills these requirements: "In a ten-room house, we always seem to congregate in the kitchen." But people often note that the limited size of this room, its location, or the presence of obstructing walls precludes the use of the kitchen as a social center for the family. In such cases, a multi-purpose room may provide an appropriate alternative.

The multi-purpose area that we are speaking of is designed in such a way that it will bring the family together for both interactive and individual tasks. The idea is to attract the family to this part of the home by having spaces in which each member can engage in a preferred activity. Separate areas must, of course, be planned for only compatible activities—mutually noninterfering ones that people enjoy performing in the presence of others. These activity zones are defined with symbolic and/or permeable boundaries to preserve an open plan that facilitates communication among people. In this way, family members are given a choice; they can enjoy each other's presence while engaging in separate activities or come together in the social spaces provided for them. Interaction is, therefore, noncontrived; people feel as if they're doing things together because they want to. We had an occasion to design such a room, which provided a family of five with individual spaces (for example, for reading, exercise, enjoying plants, etc.) and a communal area consisting of an adjustable-height table and back-rest pillows.

Preferred Environmental Characteristics

In order for the spaces that we have spoken of to be successful, they must be designed with certain characteristics that create a friendly atmosphere, increase interaction, make it comfortable to be with others, and foster group identity. Relevant design concepts are presented below along with associated explanations and supporting research.

Environmental stimulation

Mehrabian (1976) concludes from his research on the relationship between environmental characteristics and affiliation that "moderately high
arousal levels are needed for people to socialize with one another" (p. 84).
Being sociable requires activity, attentiveness, and a certain amount of effort. Social areas should, therefore, be designed to be stimulating (see
Chapter 7: Stimulation Seeking/Environmental Stimulation). In fact, as
Mehrabian has pointed out, one of the reasons that people often prefer to
socialize in the kitchen is that it is often brightly lit, contains cooking odors,
and may offer a natural view through a backyard window—factors that
contribute to our overall arousal level.

Aesthetics

When other people are encountered in aesthetically pleasing environments, the positive feelings elicited by the setting get conditioned to the
people themselves. Therefore, we tend to perceive other people more positively (Maslow and Mintz, 1956; Wollen and Montagne, 1981) and have a
greater desire to affiliate with them (Russell and Mehrabian, 1978) in attractive places than in unattractive ones. These research results seem to be
corroborated by the experiences of several of our subjects. One person
noted a decline in affiliation as room aesthetics decreased: "My family
doesn't spend as much time together in the living room as it used to; some
improvements need to be made to restore its warmth." Another individual
reported that the social center of the home became "much more inviting"
after it had been "remodeled and refurnished" with "rich golds and browns,
new carpeting, and a gorgeous hutch filled with vases, statues, and
knickknacks." Generally, it appears that people respond favorably to a
variety of improvements in room decor; however, maximally effective aesthetic designs will result from a consideration of the factors that influence
individual differences in aesthetic response (see Chapter 8). Aesthetic preferences of all family members should be considered and integrated into the
design of the social area, given that our design goal is to increase family
cohesiveness.

Family displays

Altman and Chemers (1980) noted that displays of family unity are
often found in communal areas of the American home: "In living or family

rooms one might see photographs of family members and ancestors, trophies and mementos depicting the achievements and history of family members, the best furnishings and dishes" (p. 194). These displays, and others of a similar nature (see Chapter 5: Nurturance/Displays), serve as reminders of family identity and may set the stage for conversations that strengthen family bonds even further.

Living things

As a species, we evolved in the natural environment. For this reason wilderness psychologists have argued that exposure to nature is therapeutic, representing a return to our evolutionary home. It is also true that "during evolutionary development the human species probably functioned in small groups, each member knowing the others personally" (Dubos, 1968, p. 154). Accordingly, it is quite "natural" for us to respond to each other in a caring, trusting, and sensitive manner when we gather in small groups in a natural setting.

Perhaps we can simulate our evolutionary environment by bringing nature into the home as we have argued throughout this book. Alternatively, a caring natural setting for the family may be located in an outdoor space adjacent to the home, as designers typically consider outdoor areas a part of the overall interior design job.

Recently, we have been hearing quite a bit about pet therapy for solitary individuals. People who are relatively deprived of close human contact (for example, the elderly) can experience companionship and affection in a relationship with an animal. It is also true that a pet can act as a social facilitator, softening our interactions with others. Therefore, we recommend that family spaces include areas for pets. Attention should be given to spatial requirements, furnishings, fabrics, and floor coverings so that family members can enjoy their pets with a minimum of hassle.

Warmth/comfort

Color, lighting, and furnishings should combine to create an atmosphere of warmth and friendliness. The following contrast in feelings, evoked by a family room from a previous dwelling and the present home as a whole, provides a good illustration of this dimension:

At that time, we . . . chose rather deep, warm colors. Our family room was all in tones of orange and brown. It was very large, with a corner fireplace. The carpet was a very deep pile, in a burnt-orange color. The walls were also paneled in walnut, with many built-in bookcases to suit my library. The furniture was a dark Naugahyde, deep and comfortable. The room was full of art works that we had collected over the years. It had a warm, comfortable feeling, and was by far my favorite place. There is no place in this [current] house that has such a warm feeling although I think the living room could be given such an atmosphere with appropriate decorations and furnishings. . . . Up to now this house conveys a rather sterile feeling to me. It desperately needs art work on the walls. . . . The house, up to this time, is not very inviting. It's more like an apartment . . . and not like a home.

Windows

One common method used in interior design research is to have subjects rate drawings of room interiors as particular environmental characteristics are systematically varied. Employing this procedure, Kaye and Murray (1982) found that people evaluate rooms as being more friendly and more inviting when a window is present than when it is absent. This friendliness effect also seems to be related to the size of the window and/or the view permitted (Wools, 1970).

There are a number of reasons that may account for these results: Windows provide contact with nature, access to sources of varied stimulation, and expanded visual space. Although the exact mechanism has not as yet been determined; it is clear, from interviews such as the following, that large windows should be included in family interaction spaces if possible.

[Past] We sat at a table in the dining room. The longest wall had a large window with a window seat, and I could see out onto the screened porch where the garden stood.

[Present] Our table sits in front of a sunny bay window. . . . It's a happy, sunny room. Our family sits around the table a lot.

[Future] The table would be situated in front of a large window. Under the skylight I'd like a sitting area.

Interaction foci

Designers are accustomed to creating a focal point in a room layout. However, instead of merely creating something to be looked at, the area can be furnished in order to provide a locus for family interaction.

This procedure makes sense psychologically: An object or place that provides people with a common focus (for instance, an activity to share) brings people together in a natural and comfortable way. People need not feel self-conscious as they can choose to focus on the activity, on the people, or on both (see Chapter 3: Social Withdrawal/Common or Alternate Foci). They have something in common, something to share, and something to talk about.

One of the reasons that the kitchen is a favorite family gathering area is that the act of sharing a meal together at the table provides the family with a common focus for interaction. A window supplies an interacting group with a common view. Many people, including the following, use the fireplace in the same manner:

> The fireplace, with benches on either side, was a wonderful place for family and friends to gather.

> The fireplace is located as a focal point and lends itself to the creation of a conversation center.

Certainly, a variety of other stimuli can be employed to provide families with activities to share of a passive (for example, listening to music) or a more active (for example, game playing) nature.

Circular arrangements

Square and rectangular spaces are perceptually divided into parts according to their corners and angles, whereas round shapes are seen as connected (Zeisel, 1981). Thus, if people sit in a circle they are apt to see themselves as being part of a common group with each member having equal status. These conditions are usually associated with free and open communication among group members. It's not surprising, then, that people frequently mention the presence of circular seating in favorite family interaction spaces (for example, "an oval dark mahogany table," "a round table with turned legs," and "a round low table"). People rarely mention alternative ways of defining circular spaces (for example, platforms, furnishing arrangements, floor coverings, color, lighting, etc.) although these techniques may be just as effective.

Optimal amount of space

A number of our subjects, including the following, seemed to associate close relationships with small, bounded spaces:

> *There are recessed sofas in a tiny, confined area, which I found to be friendly and conducive to conviviality.*

> *I remember being in a small room eating supper with my family.*

> *My ideal kitchen/dining area . . . would provide an intimate conversation corner.*

> *Little oases or pockets of comfort would beckon around corners.*

This association also seems to be supported by published research. Friedman (1974) found that when architecture students were asked to build models of preferred environments, the smallest and most enclosed models were built by those with the strongest interpersonal needs. Sitting in a room with a sloping ceiling is also perceived as being more friendly than sitting in a similar room with a flat roof (Wools, 1970).

All of the preceding examples seem to suggest that people may feel a common bond when they share a territory that is defined, bounded, and enclosed by some architectural or design feature (for example, walls, changes in ceiling height, partitions, etc.). However, before we develop designs for group enclosure, we must take into account two additional facts: (1) Enclosed spaces may engender feelings of crowding, and (2) Open-plan multi-purpose areas and spacious kitchens seem to be ideal for family interaction—as we have already noted. This apparent conflict between the need for enclosure and the need for space can be resolved by achieving a compromise between closeness and distance. Some solutions to this problem are discussed below.

Distance regulation.   Design can aid in the process of regulating distances between people so that they can enjoy the close presence of others without being uncomfortable. In order to accomplish this goal, however, designers must have a proper understanding of interpersonal distancing.

First of all, it appears that "there is an 'optimal range' of distance preferred by individuals and that deviations from this range, for distances judged too large or too small, result in discomfort" (Thompson, Aiello, and Epstein, 1979, p. 113). Generally speaking, people choose conversation distances that vary from about 4 to 6 feet (Scott, 1984). The concept of a *range* of comfortable distances is particularly important to keep in mind; there is no one value that is appropriate for all people and all situations. Preferred distance varies as a function of such factors as age, sex, cultural background, personality, type of relationship among people, group size, nature of the social activity, and the setting in which the interaction takes place. For example, female college students thought that a distance slightly under 4 feet was appropriate for a personal or intimate conversation between a boyfriend and girlfriend; whereas males chose distances slightly above 6 feet for more distant relationships and topics, such as classmates talking about the characteristics of a local restaurant (Scott, 1984).

Second, when people are too close to or too far away from others, they attempt to adjust the degree of closeness/distance to achieve a level of equilibrium. However, people do more than just move closer to or farther away from others. Physical proximity is only one indicator of closeness; there are also nonverbal (for example, eye contact, directness of body orientation, and angle of body lean) and verbal (for example, intimacy of the topic of conversation) signs of intimacy. These different mechanisms of varying closeness/distance from others work together as a system (for instance, one can compensate for another). For example, if we are uncomfortably close to another person physically, we can compensate by increasing nonverbal distance (for example, decreasing eye contact) or verbal distance (for example, changing the topic of conversation to a less intimate one).

But how can we facilitate this rather complex process of distance regulation in family interaction areas? Let's discuss some of the design implications. First of all, it is obvious that furniture (for example, seating and surfaces) that imposes a fixed interaction distance upon people—particularly if this distance falls outside the optimal range—will not be suitable for all people and situations. People must be given options for moving closer or farther away, physically and/or nonverbally, or else decreased affiliative behavior is likely to occur. Flexible furniture (for example, tables that expand and contract, chairs that swivel or permit different body positions, and lightweight/portable pieces) is, therefore, to be preferred. A more expensive alternative is to have alternate areas that accommodate different group sizes, preferred distances, and types of interaction.

Furthermore, because we are talking about interactions among family members, arrangements can be created that reinforce close interaction distances and touching. Corner-to-corner seating, as well as adjacent positions in a circular seating plan, allow for greater intimacy while maintaining feelings of comfort. For example, Sundstrom (1978) found that a face-to-face interaction distance of 2.5 feet was just as comfortable as an intermediate distance of 4.5 feet; but, in order to achieve the closer distance, chairs were placed at a 90° angle. It is, in fact, the indirectness of the angle of body orientation, and the natural variation in eye contact permitted by such an arrangement, that allows people who are members of a common group to enjoy a comfortable feeling of closeness with each other. The popularity of both corner-to-corner and adjacent circular seating for casual conversation among closely related individuals (reported by Sommer, 1969) is, therefore, quite understandable.

Combination of spaciousness and enclosure. One subject described an ideal room as being "spacious but cozy." This effect can be accomplished in a variety of ways depending upon the amount of available space and the nature of room layouts. For example, small, intimate spaces can be contained within a large, open area. Intimacy/enclosure is provided by sharing the small spaces with others; spaciousness is available through physical and visual access to the rest of the area. Second, a spacious room can be treated in such a manner that it is perceived as a warm, cozy environment (for example, using intimate lighting, warm colors, comfortable seating, circular arrangements, etc.). Alternatively, if space is limited—and, therefore, small enclosed areas already exist—other techniques can be employed to give the appearance of spaciousness (see Chapter 9: Freedom/Spaciousness). Attention should also be given to the distancing techniques discussed in the last section as the need for interpersonal distance becomes greater in small rooms (M. White, 1975) and enclosed areas (Tennis and Dabbs, 1975).

Guests

In addition to relating to each other on a personal basis, family members invite others into the home to take part in a variety of social activities.

The perspective that we take in this section is that, first of all, designers should be sensitive to the particular social needs of the family as a whole as well as its individual members. Second, design techniques should be used to maximize the positive aspects of social interaction and minimize its negative aspects.

Friends of Individual Family Members

According to Sebba and Churchman (1983), designers tend to conceptualize the act of entertaining guests as a public one and, therefore, create group social spaces in central, public areas of the home (for example, the living room) for that purpose. However, these researchers found that "many guests (a child's friend or a neighbor, for instance) come to visit only one member of the family" (p. 200). Communal spaces are not appropriate for these visits because of a lack of privacy; the family member and visitor may wish to be alone, but it is difficult to exclude others from the interaction in a place that belongs to all family members.

Family members prefer to entertain their own guests in areas of the home over which they exert individual control (Sebba and Churchman, 1983). However, because these areas (for example, dens and single bedrooms) are typically designed for the exclusive use of family members, it may be awkward for all people involved to have these places used for entertaining others.

These considerations suggest that designers should determine whether individual entertaining is a high priority activity for any family member(s). If so, interaction spaces may be included in the design of areas that are already under the control of these individuals. Additionally, all family members should be made aware of the dual function of these areas (for instance, solitude and private interaction with individual guests). Then, no one should feel uncomfortable about having guests taken into these private spaces. Shared bedrooms should probably not be used in this manner unless the co-owners can agree to some initially satisfactory arrangement.

These protected interaction spaces can also serve another purpose: They can be used for interactions between particular family members that require more privacy than the spaces provided for family cohesiveness. For example, one person bemoaned the fact that there was "no one good place to have a serious discussion with my husband."

Group Gatherings

The home is used for various forms of entertaining that differ according to the size of the group, the nature of the relationship among people (for instance, friends, acquaintances, and strangers), and the style of interaction (for instance, formal or informal). Clients are often quite specific about the type of entertaining that they do. Therefore, the designer's assessment of specific family entertainment needs should guide the design of social areas for guests. It is also typical for the style of entertaining to be consonant with the life style of the family, so that some of the design solutions used for satisfying the needs of family members will also function quite well for entertaining others. However, because all guests do not share the life style of their hosts or hostesses, some consideration should be given in the design of social areas to making a variety of types of people comfortable there.

Accommodating other people

When people get together, we want them to enjoy each other's company rather than feel bored, uncomfortable, or crowded. The suggestions below should be helpful in accomplishing this goal (for various group sizes and types of interaction); but, before they are presented, a further explanation of the concept of crowding is needed.

A number of events may occur when we are with others to make us feel crowded: We may experience spatial inadequacy (for example, restriction of movement and inappropriate interpersonal distances) or social constraint (for example, social pressure and a lack of privacy). In fact, any aversive event that we attribute to the presence of other people may cause us to feel crowded by them. Consequently, crowding is not just a matter of being in a crowd: We may have very pleasant experiences with a large number of others and, correspondingly, have a very negative feeling of crowding when we are with just one other person.

Space.   Entertaining people, particularly large groups, requires space so that guests do not experience feelings of spatial restriction: "My living room, which is overly filled with furniture, becomes crowded whenever we entertain." Design techniques that increase usable floor space while providing adequate seating, and allow people to regulate interpersonal distances, can help us avoid spatial problems. These techniques are particularly useful for gatherings of relative strangers, whose personal space needs are greater than those who know each other well.

Methods to increase perceived spaciousness (see Chapter 9: Freedom) can also be employed, but on a selective basis only. For example, mirrors probably wouldn't work very well in a room filled with people because the crowd would simply be reflected back, making the room appear more crowded than it really is. Light colors may increase the perceived capacity of a room, but this effect may be limited to situations where people are relatively passive. Once people start moving around and find out that space is really limited, the visual effect may be defeated. Perhaps the best of these perceived spaciousness techniques for social situations are those that provide avenues of visual escape (for example, windows and other viewing environments).

Although it is important to make sure that people are not crowded, we also do not want them to feel isolated; having too much space is just as inadequate as having too little. At parties, groups of people often gather in the rather close quarters of some kitchens, or other small spaces, and ignore more spacious areas. It is sometimes uncomfortable for people, particularly strangers, to approach each other in a large room; they may be concerned about each other's intentions. However, if people happen to find themselves close together in a small space, the situation is quite different. Because people attribute the resulting close interpersonal distances to the size limitations of the room, rather than to the motives of others, they can enjoy the close presence of other people without embarrassment. Therefore, it is advisable to include some tight spaces within the larger area used for entertaining.

Personalization. Although displays (of objects, works of art, etc.) primarily satisfy identity and aesthetic needs, the personalization of social areas also facilitates sociability and reduces feelings of social crowding. Baum and Davis (1976), using a model room technique, found that people tended to locate themselves near pictures at a cocktail party. The presence of these pictures presumably gave people the choice of either interacting with others or comfortably, and legitimately, withdrawing from interaction. The opportunity to regulate interaction in this manner is particularly welcomed at large gatherings, in which the overall level of social stimulation may be excessive at times. In such situations, accent lighting can be activated to call attention to interesting visual displays. However, these visual stimuli should not predominate to the point of distraction, as Russell and Mehrabian's (1978) research suggests that the level of affiliation with strangers may decline under such conditions.

Various forms of personalization also set the stage for interaction (Becker and Coniglio, 1975). The display of personal information (for example, about interests, goals, etc.) in social areas suggests a willingness on the part of the home owner(s) to share the self with others. This tactic puts other people at ease and stimulates an open, self-disclosing, sharing style of interaction—particularly in a small group setting. Again, however, we must caution that this approach should not be overdone; we don't want guests to feel that they are intruding into private territory.

Personalization also tends to structure interaction by suggesting appropriate topics of conversation, informing people of proper forms of behavior, and creating certain moods. Becker and Coniglio use the example of hanging a Black Power poster as a way of signaling to others how the owner wishes to be treated. A less severe message can be communicated by deliberately selecting art work for subject matter that reflects a welcoming feeling (for example, paintings of inviting landscapes, of cozy family groups, etc.). The general point to keep in mind is that we can exercise some control over the nature of social interaction that occurs at social gatherings by being sensitive to the environmental messages that are sent to others from the way we choose to personalize social areas.

Responsiveness.   If we wish to form new relationships and maintain existing ones, it is important for us to be responsive to the needs of people who are invited into the home. Guests often experience feelings of constraint, particularly when they are in unfamiliar territory and with unfamiliar people. Because these feelings may interfere with sociability, we should provide our guests with opportunities to experience both control and choice in the following ways:

1. Alternate interaction areas: In addition to—or instead of—having one main seating area, it is desirable to have a number of smaller areas that accommodate groups of different sizes (for example, a window seat for a person who wishes to take a break from social interaction, a conversational corner for two, and a small-group arrangement of pillows). The availability of these options allows people to choose the type or degree of desired interaction and, as Mehrabian (1976) points out, feel less self-conscious about approaching a particular group or leaving it.

2. Territorial definition: The boundaries of the different interaction spaces should be clearly indicated so that occupants are able to experience feelings of personal control. Desor's (1972) research also suggests that more people can be accommodated in a room that is divided into smaller territories than in a homogeneous room, before occupants begin to feel crowded. Symbolic boundary control mechanisms (for example, elevation changes, color, and objects) should probably be used so that areas are clearly defined but not closed off to people who wish to join the group.

3. Control of lighting: A lighting system should be chosen that permits people to vary the type (for example, intimate lighting for conversational corners) and the intensity of illumination. Mehrabian (1976), for example, recommends that lights should be dimmed at the beginning of a party when strangers may feel somewhat self-conscious in each other's presence and turned up later to provide sufficient arousal for interaction.

4. Flexibility in furnishings: We have already mentioned how flexible furnishings permit choice in, and control over, the type of social activity and the preferred interaction distance. Guests should also be given a choice of seating that accommodates various body types. A small person should be able to prop pillows behind the back in a seat that is too deep. A tall person should be able to stretch out. Backs should have different inclines. Rockers should be provided.

5. A welcoming environment: Many of the preferred environmental characteristics listed in the earlier section on family cohesiveness (for example, environmental stimulation, aesthetics, living things, etc.) apply equally as well to entertaining guests. The presence of these design features make guests feel that the homeowners care enough about them to create optimal conditions for an enjoyable social occasion.

Designing for characteristic interaction styles

One of the basic ways in which social situations differ is informality/ formality (Adamopoulos, 1982). Client interviews are likely to reveal a similar dichotomy in preferred styles of entertaining in the home. Designers must be sensitive to these differences and use them as guidelines for the design of areas for entertaining guests. However, the styles described below represent extremes, so that it may be appropriate in some cases to use a mixture of informal and formal design elements.

Informality. The following interview provides a good example of a preference for an informal style of entertaining. The description also contains references to some of the variables discussed below, which are responsible for the creation of an informal atmosphere.

> *The only memorable experience I can think of is sitting on the floor of the den, a small room around a low round table, having dinner with friends. All of the food was pick-up-with-your-hands-type food, and the wine was in a skin. . . . Dinner parties in the dining room, which happen rarely, are excruciatingly boring to me.*

1. Seating: Comfortable seating—which encourages people to assume lounging positions of the body, spread out, curl up, take off shoes, put up feet—is ideal. Design elements that facilitate floor seating can also be used (for example, soft floor surfaces, stacks of floor pillows, hassocks or modular pieces for back rests, and platforms). Seating arrangements should support comfortable conversation distances (4 to 6 feet).

2. Self-service: Features that allow guests to do things for themselves, rather than be waited on, make them feel at home (for example, a variety of serving carts and other surfaces arranged in close proximity to the seating so that all guests can serve themselves easily and a "guest" cabinet in the powder room containing extra towels and personal items).

3. Use of back-stage areas: People with an informal orientation to entertaining are likely to be comfortable with inviting guests into the back-stage areas of the home used for family gatherings (for example, kitchens). Guests also feel that they can "let their hair down" and relax there—by participating in meal preparation, for example: "When I entertain it's very informal, and everyone always ends up helping in the kitchen." Kitchens can be designed for people who often entertain in this manner in order to permit a number of people to work there comfortably.

4. Emotionally releasing activities: Several of our subjects mentioned that they like to entertain in "fun areas," where people can engage in enjoyable activities together. Clients can be questioned about what kinds of spaces they would like to have for this purpose (for example, a place for dancing, the old family room concept with tables for pool and/or ping pong, a technology room with computers set up for group participation, or a communal hot tub).

5. Engagement: People who wish to create an informal social atmosphere will most likely prefer an aesthetic of engagement (see Chapter 8). Basically, social areas can be designed to achieve an organic relationship with one's surroundings (for example, a piece of driftwood used as a table

base), to create a lived-in feeling (for example, soft upholstery that shows the imprint of use), and to permit guests the opportunity to manipulate the environment (for example, objects that guests can touch and handle, such as collections of sea shells). Other relevant design ideas are referred to in Chapter 8.

Formality.   Adamopoulos (1982) found a correlation between the informality of a setting and the occurrence of associative behaviors (for example, laughing with, talking with, and eating with). On the other hand, people who prefer formal entertaining styles may be more concerned with other social motives (for instance, status). The following design concepts may, therefore, be more appropriate for these individuals:

1. On-stage arrangements: In contrast to the informal style, formal entertaining requires a strict separation between private, back-stage areas and public, front regions of the home. Guests are, of course, only allowed in front rooms, where homeowners can show off their best things and appear "calm, organized, pleasant, and gracious as they go on stage" (Altman and Chemers, 1980, p. 96). Rather than being exposed to the potential confusion and disarray of the kitchen, guests are treated to a "performance" in a formal dining room, as a well-prepared and attractive meal is presented to them as if no effort were involved in its preparation. People are served and catered to—as opposed to an emphasis upon self-service—with the best china, stemware, and tableware reserved for exclusive company use.

2. Conventionality: Design elements should be chosen in order to reinforce conventional forms of behavior. The following environmental message is, then, communicated to guests: "We are rather formal here; we expect good manners and polite conversation—all of the known social graces." The orderly, "front parlor" look of the period styles would fit in well here; these styles suggest the formality, grace, and manners of an earlier era. However, contemporary designs are also applicable because similar behavioral expectations can be communicated by the forms themselves (for example, firm vs. soft, straight vs. curved, fragile collections, and fabrics whose color and/or texture suggest that they might soil easily). Conversational distance should remain within the same range that we have been advocating; however, messages of status differences (for example, rectangular tables with "head" positions and host and hostess chairs) and distance (for example, coffee-table barriers between seats) can be communicated simultaneously.

3. Impression management: Laumann and House (1970) argue "that more than any other part of the home, the living room reflects the indi-

vidual's conscious and unconscious attempts to express a social identity" (p. 190). It is the designer's role to understand the type of impression that the client wishes to present to others and facilitate its expression—but not in a superficial way that interferes with the fulfillment of other needs. Laumann and House also identified two distinct groups of individuals among their high socioeconomic-class subjects, an analysis which may assist designers in conceptualizing the status needs of their clients and selecting designs accordingly. The "traditional" group consists of nonmobile, established upper-class individuals who prefer traditional decor. Front rooms should be designed for these people in order to present a stable, comfortable, well-to-do image (for example, antiques, rich fabrics, elegant accessories, and traditional furniture styles). On the other hand, the "moderns," a group of upwardly mobile individuals whose living rooms contain such things as modern furniture and abstract art, tend to "spurn the style of the traditional upper class in favor of the newer fashions" (Laumann and House, 1970, p. 198). Perhaps some expendable design elements can be chosen for them, with the idea that they are to be replaced with other "fun designs" in the near future when the style changes. But, "conspicuous consumption must be done with 'taste'" for these people, in order to validate their "claims to high status in respects other than mere money" (Laumann and House, 1970, p. 198).

4. Aesthetic distance: People who wish to create a formal social environment will probably prefer an aesthetic of distance. An explanation of this approach, along with appropriate design examples, is presented in Chapter 8. Generally speaking, designs should be distinctive; that is, they should have the quality of being striking without violating standards of tastefulness. In this way, people can demonstrate their uniqueness, but at the same time show that they share the values of the larger community.

EPILOGUE

Throughout this book we have advocated a person-oriented, need-centered approach to residential interior design. Thus, in order to make meaningful recommendations concerning the design of interior space, we must, at first, understand what people do in their homes (that is, what important psychological needs are fulfilled there). We have also attempted to supply our readers with a framework for organizing information about the relationship between people and the home environment. Accordingly, we have conceptualized the home as a setting that presents opportunities for, or obstacles to, the satisfaction of nine psychological needs: control, privacy, identity, security, order, variety, aesthetics, choice, and sociability.

Our view of the person in the home environment is, of course, much more complex than that. For example, the fact that people try to achieve privacy at home is certainly not new information. However, research and theory in the field of environmental psychology have suggested that privacy may mean different things to different people or different things to the same person at different times. Privacy may mean maintaining control over personal information. That information may be visual, acoustic, or some combination of the two. Privacy may also mean minimizing interference from others. Sources of interference may also vary (for example, visual distractions, noise, or intrusions). Additionally, the desire for privacy may signify a need to get away from others temporarily through either physical or psychological withdrawal. And, finally, when people say they want privacy, they may mean that they wish to regulate social interaction so that they can achieve a balance between social contact and solitude. Because each variety of privacy may require a unique design solution, it is necessary for us to go beyond the mere identification of the presence of a need. We must also try to understand what particular form this need takes for this individual at this time. (This strategy should be followed for the other needs as well, as long as they appear as dominant themes in the client interview.)

Of course, need-assessment is only the first stage of the approach we are suggesting, as design guidelines must be derived from an understanding of the dynamics of need-satisfaction. Throughout the book we have presented such guidelines in the form of design concepts. Each form of each need is accompanied by a number of these concepts (for example, the use of windows, surrogate views, and common foci to facilitate psychological withdrawal). However, the successful application of these concepts requires a skilled designer, who must translate a conceptual design into a concrete one that fits the personal, situational, and spatial requirements of the client. We have only given a few examples of specific design elements—just enough to clearly define each concept. Furthermore, specific design solutions must undergo evaluation in order to determine whether they are meeting the needs for which they were intended, a course of action that requires some sort of client follow-up.

The design process as we have outlined it seems to necessitate an interdisciplinary approach. Few of us have sufficient training in both the areas of environmental psychology and interior design to be able to deal with the complex challenges that are provided by each field. In fact, this book could not have been written without such interdisciplinary cooperation. We would, therefore, like to encourage the formation of working relationships between psychologists and designers. Communication may, at first, be difficult as people trained in different disciplines tend to speak different languages. But after this initial problem is solved, we have found that the rewards of the creative synthesis of fields far outweigh the costs. And, most importantly, the real beneficiaries of this approach are the people who enlist the services of a team of psychologist/design professionals who are able to create personal environments that respond to the totality of needs of the individual.

BIBLIOGRAPHY

Adamopoulos, J. (1982). The perception of interpersonal behavior. *Environment and Behavior, 14,* 29–44.

Alschuler, R., and Hattwick, L. (1947). *Painting and personality.* Chicago: University of Chicago Press.

Altman, I. (1975). *The environment and social behavior.* Monterey, CA: Brooks/Cole.

Altman, I., and Chemers, M. (1980). *Culture and environment.* Monterey, CA: Brooks/Cole.

Arnheim, R. (1954). *Art and visual perception.* Berkeley, CA: University of California Press.

Baron, R.M., Mandel, D.R., Adams, C.A., and Griffen, L.M. (1976). Effects of social density in university residential environments. *Journal of Personality and Social Psychology, 34,* 434–46.

Baum, A., and Davis, G.E. (1976). Spatial and social aspects of crowding perception. *Environment and Behavior, 8,* 527–44.

Bechtel, R.B. (1977). *Enclosing behavior.* Stroudsburg, PA: Dowden, Hutchinson and Ross.

Becker, F.D. (1981). *Workspace.* New York: Praeger.

Becker, F.D., and Coniglio, C. (1975). Environmental messages: Personalization and territory. *Humanitas, 11,* 55–74.

Berrill, N.J. (1955). *Man's emerging mind.* New York: Dodd, Mead.

Berleant, A. (1982). The viewer in the landscape. In P. Bart, A. Chen, and G. Francescato, eds., *Knowledge for design* (pp. 161–65). Washington, D.C.: Environmental Design Research Association.

Berlyne, D.E., ed. (1974). *Studies in the new experimental aesthetics: Steps toward an objective psychology of aesthetic appreciation.* New York: Halsted.

Berman, C. (1980, March/April). Tuning for sound: Wisely-chosen surfaces heighten acoustical efficiency. *Residential Interiors,* pp. 110–11.

Brehm, J. (1966). *A theory of psychological reactance.* New York: Academic Press.

Cooper, C. (1970). The house as symbol of the self. In H.M. Proshansky, W.H. Ittelson, and L.G. Rivlin, eds., *Environmental psychology: Man and his physical setting* (pp. 435–48). New York: Holt, Rinehart and Winston.

Crane, C. (1982). *Personal places: How to make your home your own.* New York: Whitney Library of Design.

Cunningham, M.R. (1977). Notes on the psychological basis of environmental design: The right-left dimension in apartment floor plans. *Environment and Behavior, 9,* 125–35.

deCharms, R. (1968). *Personal causation: The internal affective determinants of behavior.* New York: Academic Press.

Delprato, D.J. (1977). Promoting electrical energy conservation in commercial users. *Environment and Behavior, 9,* 433–40.

Desor, J.A. (1972). Toward a psychological theory of crowding. *Journal of Personality and Social Psychology, 21,* 79–83.

Dobbin, M. (1983, December 11). Computers come home for good. *The Baltimore Sun,* pp. F1–F2.

Dubos, R. (1968). *So human an animal.* New York: Scribner.

Edney, J.J. (1976). Human territories: Comment on functional properties. *Environment and Behavior, 1,* 31–47.

Edney, J.J., and Buda, M.A. (1976). Distinguishing territoriality and privacy: Two studies. *Human Ecology, 4,* 283–95.

Eliovson, S. (1978). The Japanese garden. In S. Kaplan and R. Kaplan, eds., *Humanscape: Environments for people* (pp. 170–74). North Scituate, MA: Duxbury.

Evans, G.W., and Lovell, B. (1979). Design modification in an open-plan school. *Journal of Educational Psychology, 71,* 41–49.

Farrenkopf, T., and Roth, V. (1980). The university faculty office as an environment. *Environment and Behavior, 12,* 467–77.

Findlay, R.A., and Field, K.F. (1982). Functional roles of visual complexity in user perceptions of architecture. In P. Bart, A. Chen, and G. Francescato, eds., *Knowledge for design* (pp. 145–53). Washington, D.C.: Environmental Design Research Association.

Fiske, D.W., and Maddi, S.R., eds. (1961). *Functions of varied experience.* Homewood, IL: Dorsey.

Flynn, J.E., Spencer, T.J., Martyniuk, O., and Hendrick, C. (1973). Interim study of procedures for investigating the effect of light on impression and behavior. *Journal of the Illuminating Engineering Society, 3,* 87–94.

Friedman, S. (1974). Relationships among cognitive complexity, interpersonal dimension, and spatial preferences and propensities. In S. Friedman and J.B. Juhasz, eds., *Environments: Notes and selections on objects, spaces, and behavior* (pp. 101–6). Monterey, CA: Brooks/Cole.

Goffman, E. (1959). *The presentation of self in everyday life.* New York: Doubleday.

Hall, E.T. (1966). *The hidden dimension.* New York: Doubleday.

Hansen, W.B., and Altman, I. (1976). Decorating personal places. *Environment and Behavior, 8,* 491–504.

Hershberger, R.G. (1970). A study of meaning and architecture. In H. Sanoff and S. Cohn, eds., *Proceedings of the 1st Annual Environmental Design Research Association Conference* (pp. 86–100). Stroudsburg, PA: Dowden, Hutchinson and Ross.

High, T., and Sundstrom, E. (1977). Room flexibility and space use in a dormitory. *Environment and Behavior, 9,* 81–90.

Hill, A.R. (1970). Visibility and privacy. In D.V. Canter, ed., *Architectural psychology* (pp. 39–43). London: RIBA.

Holahan, C.J. (1982). *Environmental psychology.* New York: Random House.

Ittelson, W.H., Rivlin, L.G., and Proshansky, H.M. (1970). The use of behavioral maps in environmental psychology. In H.M. Proshansky, W.H. Ittelson, and L.G. Rivlin, eds., *Environmental psychology: Man and his physical setting* (pp. 658–68). New York: Holt, Rinehart and Winston.

Jackson, D. (1967). *Personality research form manual.* Goshen, NY: Research Psychologists Press.

Kaplan, R. (1973). Some psychological benefits of gardening. *Environment and Behavior, 5,* 145–62.

Kaplan, S. (1975). An informal model for the prediction of preference. In E.H. Zube, R.O. Brush, and J.G. Fabos, eds., *Landscape assessment: Value, perceptions, and resources* (pp. 92–101). Stroudsburg, PA: Dowden, Hutchinson and Ross.

Kaplan, S., and Kaplan, R. (1978). *Humanscape: Environments for people.* North Scituate, MA: Duxbury.

Kaplan, S., Kaplan, R., and Wendt, J.S. (1972). Rated preference and complexity for natural and urban visual material. *Perception and Psychophysics, 12,* 354–56.

Kaye, S.M., and Murray, M.A. (1982). Evaluations of an architectural space as a function of variations in furniture arrangement, furniture density, and windows. *Human Factors, 24*, 609–18.

Ladd, F.C. (1976, September). *Housing, neighborhoods and self-esteem: Toward equal opportunity in residential environments.* Paper presented at the meeting of the American Psychological Association, Washington, D.C.

Lang, J. (1982). Symbolic aesthetics in architecture: Toward a research agenda. In P. Bart, A. Chen, and G. Francescato, eds., *Knowledge for design* (pp. 172–82). Washington, D.C.: Environmental Design Research Association.

Langer, E.J., and Rodin, J. (1976). The effects of choice and enhanced personal responsibility for the aged: A field experiment in an institutional setting. *Journal of Personality and Social Psychology, 34*, 191–98.

Laumann, E.O., and House, J.S. (1970). Living room styles and social attributes: The patterning of material artifacts in a modern urban community. In E.O. Laumann, P.M. Siegal, and R.W. Hodge, eds., *The logic of social hierarchies* (pp. 189–203). Chicago: Markham.

Leff, H.L. (1978). *Experience, environment, and human potentials.* New York: Oxford University Press.

Lynch, K. (1960). *The image of the city.* Cambridge, MA: M.I.T. Press.

Maddi, S.R., Charlens, A.M., Maddi, M., and Smith, A.J. (1962). Effects of monotony and novelty on imaginative productions. *Journal of Personality, 30*, 513–27.

Mandel, D.R., Baron, R.M., and Fisher, J.D. (1980). Room utilization and dimensions of density: Effects of height and view. *Environment and Behavior, 12*, 308–19.

Margulis, S.T. (1979). *Privacy as information management: A social psychological and environmental framework* (Report No. 79–1793). Washington, D.C.: National Bureau of Standards.

Maslow, A.H. (1954). *Motivation and personality.* New York: Harper.

Maslow, A.H., and Mintz, N.C. (1956). Effects of aesthetic surroundings: I. Initial short-term effects of three aesthetic conditions upon perceiving "energy" and "well-being" in faces. *Journal of Psychology, 41*, 247–54.

McKechnie, G.E. (1977). The environmental response inventory in application. *Environment and Behavior, 9*, 255–76.

Mehrabian, A. (1976). *Public places and private spaces: The psychology of work, play, and living environments.* New York: Basic Books.

Mehrabian, A., and Russell, J.A. (1973). A measure of arousal seeking tendency. *Environment and Behavior, 5*, 315–33.

_____. (1974a). *An approach to environmental psychology*. Cambridge, MA: M.I.T. Press.

_____. (1974b). A verbal measure of information rate for studies in environmental psychology. *Environment and Behavior, 6*, 233–52.

_____. (1975). Environmental effects on affiliation among strangers. *Humanities, 11*, 219–30.

Miller, S. (1981). Coping with crowding in an elevator: Staring at the floor numbers is not enough. In A.E. Osterberg, C.P. Tiernan, and R.A. Findlay, eds., *Design research interactions* (pp. 235–40). Washington, D.C.: Environmental Design Research Association.

Miller, T.L. (1978). Behavioral and spatial change in response to an altered behavior setting. *Environmental Psychology and Nonverbal Behavior, 3*, 23–42.

Mintz, N.L. (1956). Effects of aesthetic surroundings: II. Prolonged and repeated experience in a "beautiful" and an "ugly" room. *Journal of Psychology, 41*, 459–66.

Moos, R.H. (1976). *The human context: Environmental determinants of behavior*. New York: Wiley.

Osborne, H. (1970). *The art of appreciation*. New York: Oxford University Press.

Pearson, P.H. (1970). Relationships between global and specified measures of novelty seeking. *Journal of Consulting and Clinical Psychology, 34*, 199–204.

Peterson, R., Wekerle, G.R., and Morley, D. (1978). Women and environments: An overview of an emerging field. *Environment and Behavior, 10*, 511–34.

Platt, J.R. (1961). Pattern and change. In D.W. fiske and S.R. Maddi, eds., *Functions of varied experience* (pp. 402–30). Homewood, IL: Dorsey.

Proshansky, H.M. (1978). The city and self-identity. *Environment and Behavior, 10*, 147–69.

Proshansky, H.M., Ittelson, W.H., and Rivlin, L.G. (1970). Freedom of choice and behavior in a physical setting. In H.M. Proshansky, W.H. Ittelson, and L.G. Rivlin, eds., *Environmental psychology: Man and his physical setting* (pp. 173–83). New York: Holt, Rinehart and Winston.

Rapoport, A., and Kantor, R.E. (1976). Complexity and ambiguity in environmental design. *Journal of the American Institute of Planners, 33*, 210–21.

Raschko, B.B. (1982). *Housing interiors for the disabled and elderly.* New York: Van Nostrand Reinhold.

Rooney, W.F. (1980). *Practical guide to home lighting.* New York: Bantam/Hudson Idea Books.

Rossman, B.B., and Ulehla, Z.J. (1977). Psychological reward values associated with wilderness use. *Environment and Behavior, 9,* 41–67.

Russell, J.A., and Mehrabian, A. (1978). Approach-avoidance and affiliation as functions of the emotion-eliciting quality of an environment. *Environment and Behavior, 10,* 355–87.

Russell, J.A., and Pratt, G. (1980). A description of the affective quality attributed to environments. *Journal of Personality and Social Psychology, 38,* 311–22.

Sadalla, E.K., and Oxley, D. (1984). The perception of room size: The rectangularity illusion. *Environment and Behavior, 16,* 394–405.

Samuelson, D.J., and Lindauer, M.S. (1976). Perception, evaluation, and performance in a neat and messy room by high and low sensation seekers. *Environment and Behavior, 8,* 291–306.

Savinar, J. (1975). The effect of ceiling height on personal space. *Man-Environment Systems, 5,* 321–24.

Schiffenbauer, A.I., Brown, J.E., Perry, P.L., Shulack, L.K., and Zanzola, A.M. (1977). The relationship between density and crowding: Some architectural modifiers. *Environment and Behavior, 9,* 3–14.

Scott, J.A. (1984). Comfort and seating distance in living rooms: The relationship of interactants and topic of conversation. *Environment and Behavior, 16,* 35–54.

Seal, D.J., and Sylvester, G.E. (1982). Optimizing working conditions for the software employee. In P. Bart, A. Chen, and G. Francescato, eds., *Knowledge for design* (pp. 406–14). Washington, D.C.: Environmental Design Research Association.

Sebba, R., and Churchman, A. (1983). Territories and territoriality in the home. *Environment and Behavior, 15,* 191–210.

Sharpe, D.T. (1975). *The psychology of color and design.* Totowa, NJ: Littlefield/Adams.

Sommer, R. (1969). *Personal space: The behavioral basis of design.* Englewood Cliffs, NJ: Prentice-Hall.

_____. (1974). *Tight spaces: Hard architecture and how to humanize it.* Englewood Cliffs, NJ: Prentice-Hall.

Sommer, R., and Olsen, H. (1980). The soft classroom. *Environment and Behavior, 12,* 3–16.

Stokols, D. (1976). The experience of crowding in primary and secondary environments. *Environment and Behavior, 8,* 49–86.

Sundstrom, E. (1978). A test of equilibrium theory: Effects of topic intimacy and proximity on verbal and nonverbal behavior in pairs of friends and strangers. *Environmental Psychology and Nonverbal Behavior, 3,* 3–16.

Sundstrom, E., and Sundstrom, M.G. (1983). *Work places: Psychology of the physical environment in offices and factories.* Monterey, CA: Brooks/Cole.

Taylor, S.M., and Konrad, V.A. (1980). Scaling dispositions toward the past. *Environment and Behavior, 12,* 283–307.

Tennis, G.H., and Dabbs, J.M. (1975). Sex, setting, and personal space: First grade through college. *Sociometry, 38,* 385–94.

Thomas, J.C. (1977). *Cognitive psychology from the perspective of wilderness survival* (Research Rep. No. 6647–28603). Yorktown Heights, NY: IBM Thomas J. Watson Research Laboratory.

Thompson, D.E., Aiello, J.R., and Epstein, Y.M. (1979). Interpersonal distance preferences. *Journal of Nonverbal Behavior, 4,* 113–18.

Toffler, A. (1970). *Future shock.* New York: Random House.

Tognoli, J., and Horwitz, J. (1982). From childhood home to adult home: Environmental transformations. In P. Bart, A. Chen, and G. Francescato, eds., *Knowledge for design* (pp. 321–28). Washington, D.C.: Environmental Design Research Association.

Ulrich, R.S. (1981). Natural versus urban scenes: Some psychological effects. *Environment and Behavior, 13,* 523–56.

Verderber, S.F. (1982). Designing for the therapeutic functions of windows in the hospital rehabilitation environment. In P. Bart, A. Chen, and G. Francescato, eds., *Knowledge for design* (pp. 476–92). Washington, D.C.: Environmental Design Research Association.

Weale, M.J., Croake, J.W., and Weale, W.B. (1982). *Environmental interiors.* New York: Macmillan.

Weisner, T.S., and Weibel, J.C. (1981). Home environments and family lifestyles in California. *Environment and Behavior, 13,* 417–60.

Westin, A. (1970). *Privacy and freedom.* New York: Atheneum.

Wexner, L.B. (1954). The degree to which colors (hues) are associated with mood-tones. *Journal of Applied Psychology, 38,* 432–35.

White, M. (1975). Interpersonal distance as affected by room size, status, and sex. *The Journal of Social Psychology, 95,* 241–49.

White, R.W. (1959). Motivation reconsidered: The concept of competence. *Psychological Review, 66,* 297–333.

Wohlwill, J.F. (1974). Human response to levels of environmental stimulation. *Human Ecology, 2,* 127–47.

Wolfe, M., and Laufer, R. (1975). The concept of privacy in childhood and adolescence. In D.H. Carson, ed., *Man-environment interactions: Evaluations and applications: Part II, Vol. 6. Privacy,* S.T. Margulis, vol. ed., (pp. 29–54). Stroudsburg, PA: Dowden, Hutchinson & Ross.

Wollen, D.D., and Montagne, M. (1981). College classroom environment: Effects of sterility versus amiability on student and teacher performance. *Environment and Behavior, 13,* 707–16.

Wools, R.M. (1970). The assessment of room friendliness. In D.V. Canter, ed., *Architectural psychology* (pp. 48–55). London: RIBA.

Zeisel, J. (1981). *Inquiry by design: Tools for environment-behavior research.* Monterey, CA: Brooks/Cole.

Zuckerman, M., Kolin, E.A., Price, L., and Zoob, I. (1964). Development of a sensation-seeking scale. *Journal of Consulting Psychology, 28,* 477–82.

INDEX

173

ABOUT THE AUTHORS

Stuart Miller is professor of psychology at Towson State University and a consultant to IDEA Associates, a firm providing interior design and environmental analysis services to residential, professional, and executive clients.

Dr. Miller has published widely in the areas of experimental, social, and environmental psychology. His articles have appeared in the *Journal of Experimental Psychology, Psychonomic Science,* the *Journal of Applied Social Psychology,* and *Environmental Psychology and Nonverbal Behavior.*

Dr. Miller holds a B.S. and a Ph.D. from the University of Maryland and an M.A. from Hollins College.

Judith K. Schlitt—a professional member of the American Society of Interior Designers—heads IDEA Associates, is a faculty member of the Parsons School of Design, and recently created and produced her own television series on interior design for American Cablesystems.

Ms. Schlitt regularly presents and participates in programs for the American Society of Interior Designers, the Environmental Design Research Association, the Association for the Study of Man-Environment Relations, and the New York Designers Lighting Forum—in which she also holds memberships. Her commentaries on design have been widely published; and she has been the subject, along with her work, of numerous articles in the news media.

Ms. Schlitt, a graduate of the Parsons School of Design, studied psychology at the New School for Social Research and environmental psychology at the State University of New York at Purchase.